Smooth Talkers
The Linguistic Performance of Auctioneers and Sportscasters

Everyday Communication: Case Studies of Behavior in Context

Wendy Leeds-Hurwitz & Stuart J. Sigman, Series Editors

Smooth Talkers
The Linguistic Performance of Auctioneers and Sportscasters

Koenraad Kuiper
University of Canterbury

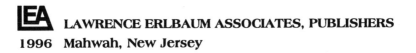
LAWRENCE ERLBAUM ASSOCIATES, PUBLISHERS
1996   Mahwah, New Jersey

P
95
.K85
Krb

Lawrence Erlbaum Associates, Inc., Publishers
10 Industrial Avenue
Mahwah, New Jersey 07430

cover design by Mairav Salomon-Dekel

Library of Congress Cataloging-in-Publication Data

Kuiper, Koenraad.
     Smooth talkers / Koenraad Kuiper
        p.   cm.
     Includes bibliographical references and index.
     ISBN 0-8058-1719-0 (alk. paper). — ISBN 0-8058-1720-4 (pbk.
: alk. paper)
       1. Oral communication.   2. Auctioneers—Language.   3.
Sportscasters—Language. 4. Speech. I. Title.
P95.K85 1996
302.2'242—dc20   95-409
                                               CIP

Books published by Lawrence Erlbaum Associates are printed on acid-free paper and their bindings are chosen for strength and durability.

Printed in the United States of America
10 9 8 7 6 5 4 3 2 1

Dedicated to the memory of
Philippa Constance Flavell
1949–1989
in affectionate memory, and acknowledgment of
her interest in
the ways people acquire knowledge.

Contents

Editors' Preface

The Everyday Communication series is devoted to the publication of case studies concerning patterns of human communication behavior placed within relevant cultural and social contexts. Each monograph within the series is intended to illuminate our understanding of the relationship between communication and context, and to do so with data collected through a variety of naturalistic methods.

This first monograph, *Smooth Talkers: The Linguistic Performance of Auctioneers and Sportscasters*, evidences the flexibility with which we have attempted to proceed with this editorial mission. Although most of the monographs in the series will describe data drawn from a single context, Koenraad Kuiper's research is based on data from two distinct social situations—racecourse broadcasts and auctions—and from several countries—Australia, England, New Zealand, and the United States. Strictly speaking, there is no singular situation around which the analysis revolves. From this vantage point, then, Kuiper's work may at first appear as an odd choice to inaugurate this series. We think not.

Smooth Talkers provides a rich linguistic analysis of some features of context that characterize many everyday social situations and of the consequences of these features for participants' communication performances. In other words, Kuiper attempts to delve below the surface of two particular communication situations in the hopes of discovering regularities that bind a host of situations. The particular feature studied by Kuiper is "cognitive complexity," the type and amount of processing pressure placed on speakers' short-term memory. Kuiper's thesis is that certain communication contexts place an inordinate pressure on speakers to observe what is transpiring around them, to place these observations in short-term memory, and to formulate speech reports or announcements about what was observed. In order to accommodate the rapid speech processing demands placed on such communicators as racecourse announcers and auctioneers, communities develop repertoires of formulae (i.e., whole linguistic units that are usually larger than single words and that are used intact). These repertoires enable speakers to engage in unusually rapid cognitive processing of messages by having reports and announcements fit into standardized formats.

The contribution of this analysis of the speech of "smooth talkers" is twofold: first, the monograph demonstrates how a linguistic hypothesis can be tested via comparative methods. Kuiper does not simply describe the speech of one group of smooth talkers, people who are caught in high-demand situations and who nonetheless speak rapidly; rather, he has generated data from a series of situations that can be arrayed on a continuum from high to low processing pressure. This permits a test of his premise that, as processing demands increase, so does the presence of oral formulae. Thus, Kuiper goes beyond description into the realm of explanation. This is so rarely attempted in qualitative research that we are pleased to include this monograph in our series for that reason alone. Yet Kuiper provides more.

The second contribution of Kuiper's monograph results from his decision to situate this work in the literature on oral performance more generally. Citing the work of Parry and Lord, and echoing that of Walter Ong, Kuiper suggests that much of spoken communication is formulaic. Formulaic linguistic units permit speakers to respond to and communicate about novel circumstances and contexts with an economy of speech processing effort. What is particularly revealing about Kuiper's analysis is that it focuses not on such traditional domains of orality as narrative, but on such mundane and apparently ephemeral events as auctioneering and sports commentating. Further, according to Kuiper, much of everyday oral performance is routine; it could not be otherwise—for without formulae we would not be able to process speech as rapidly as we do, and we would not be able to signal the difference between new and expected information as concisely.

In brief, *Smooth Talkers* provides interesting data on two naturally occurring contexts—racecourse announcing and auctioneering—and, in the process, offers a perspective on a feature of communication undergirding most everyday contexts.

Wendy Leeds-Hurwitz
Stuart J. Sigman

Note

Because almost all sports commentators and auctioneers are male, almost all the speakers whose speech was recorded and transcribed for this book are male. Sports commentators and auctioneers are predominantly male for a variety of social, cultural, and historical reasons not related to male and female capacities for speech but because of gender role assignment. Women could be auctioneers, sports commentators, or oral heroic poets, and, in a few places, they are.

This places me in a quandary about current imperatives to use gender-neutral terminology and, especially, gender-neutral pronouns. Where I am speaking about a particular male speaker, or a group of speakers who are male, I have sometimes used the pronoun "he." I have also chosen to use both plural and singular "they." Singular "they" has a long and honorable history and is used frequently in speech for a gender-neutral singular (Zanetti, 1991).

Acknowledgments

Many people have played a part in creating this monograph. The people who have had the most impact on it have been the performers themselves. Without the high levels of professional skill of auctioneers like Alistair Hopkinson of Pyne Gould Guinness; Fred Fowler, formerly of Dalgety's and now of Pyne Gould Guinness, Canterbury, New Zealand; Rod Cameron of Wrightson NMA; Douglas Bilodeau of Douglas Galleries, Deerfield, Massachusetts; Hank Currin and Earl Capps of Fuquay-Varina, North Carolina; Milt Crosby, auctioneer for the Whately Cooperative Livestock Auction in Massachusetts; commentators of *Hockey Night in Canada* such as Bill Hewitt, Danny Gallivan, Dick Irvine, Bob Cole, and Gary Dornhoefer; and racing commentator Reon Murtha, I would not have developed an interest in formulaic speech. Some of the performers in this book have talked at length to me about their craft and I gratefully acknowledge their help. They include race caller Reon Murtha and auctioneers Richard "Dickie" Bell, Douglas Bilodeau, Hank Currin, Alistair Hopkinson, and L.A. "Speed" Riggs.

My students helped over the years to further my interests. Douglas Haggo, in particular, helped with his meticulous observations and careful prosodic transcriptions. Our four joint papers form the foundation work for this study. Paddy Austin made a first sortie into the speech of race callers with me. For the work dealing with the social context of formulaic speech I have to thank my students: Marie Flindall, Francesca Hickey, Ji Feng Yuan, Shu Xiaogu, Joan Smith, and Daphne Tan, with whom I did joint research on the formulaic speech of their and my cultures. Peter Kane helped with the transcription of racing commentaries. Rosemary Hind searched for useful material in the traditional scholarship on oral formulaic performance. Frederick Tillis of the University of Massachusetts at Amherst helped with musical analysis and commentary on the speech of the tobacco auctioneers. Joseph Clark Robert, of the University of Richmond, Virginia, answered some of my questions about the tobacco industry.

For financial and practical assistance I am grateful to the New Zealand University Grants Committee and the University of Canterbury for research grants, and to the University of Canterbury for periods of study leave. The New Zealand–U.S. Educational Foundation provided a Fulbright Hays Travel Award that allowed me time in the United States to place my work before a wider critical audience and to check some hypotheses from earlier periods of research. I am grateful to Radio New Zealand, Dave Roberts of CBC Radio, Geoffrey Miller of Kingston, New York, Billy Yeargin of Oxford, North Carolina, and the R. J. Reynolds Tobacco Corporation for making recordings available to me.

A number of people provided hospitality of various kinds while the field work for this study was conducted. In that regard I have to thank Rowland and Mary Burdon, Brenda Follmer of the R. J. Reynolds Tobacco Company, Dr. Heinz Seltmann of North Carolina State University, and Professor Michele Dominy of Red Hook, New York.

Some of what is in this book has appeared in earlier forms in various journals and collections of papers. Permission to reprint and adapt such material is acknowledged from the following journals: *American Speech, Language in Society, Linguistics,* and *Oral Tradition,* and from the editors of Bell and Holmes (1990).

For critical comment and collegial encouragement I am grateful to John Andreae, Derek Davy, Michele Dominy, Janet Holmes, and Andrew Pawley.

Allan Bell and Alison Kuiper gave valuable editorial advice that helped to make the text a clearer one, as did the editors of the series in which this monograph is published. I am similarly grateful to them. For those failings that remain, I take sole responsibility.

1

Introduction

Smooth talkers come in many guises and are to be found in many places. Storytellers entertain their friends in the corners of pubs and bars. Encyclopedia salesmen and Jehovah's Witnesses produce fluent testimony for their products and beliefs. In auction rooms and livestock yards auctioneers produce uninterrupted streams of speech, and behind microphones at sporting events commentators entertain thousands and sometimes millions of fans. Each one is thoroughly at home with his or her variety of speech and yet sometimes incapable of similarly fluent speech in other circumstances.

This book looks at the speech of sportscasters and auctioneers. They are smooth talkers of a distinctive kind in that they use characteristic techniques in order to speak fluently. These techniques allow them to become extraordinarily fluent beyond the levels achieved by most other speakers. This book first examines the contexts in which sportscasters and auctioneers speak and the nature of their speech. It then offers a set of theories to explain how this speech comes to be the way it is. These theories might be testable in the laboratory, but instead, in this study, they are tested in the real world by looking for conditions that should be conducive to smooth talking, and then recording, transcribing, and analyzing the speech produced in such circumstances.

This research began as purely linguistic research but has become increasingly interdisciplinary. Writers such as Popper (1965) and Newton-Smith (1981) wrote that phenomena in themselves lead nowhere in particular and that the appearance that they do is an illusion. I believe them. But my belief has been constantly undermined by the speakers themselves and by the way the research tracks have fanned out. Richard Bauman (1986) helped by suggesting that:

> In the light of all these concurrent and potentially complementary inquiries into form, function, and conduct of oral narration, the need appears all the more compelling for a fusion of various separate lines of investigation that have engaged the interest of the respective disciplines. (p. 144)

This book attempts to follow Bauman's advice. In purely linguistic terms this is a study of what Noam Chomsky (1965) called *performance*, that is the *use* of

1

language rather than the structure of language itself. The latter he termed *competence.* In Chomsky's sense of the word *performance,* human beings perform all the time. They perform tasks ranging from private ones like brushing their teeth to socially visible and politically significant tasks like addressing protest rallies outside the White House. This book is about performance through speech.

There are many frameworks that are used for studying such performance. It can be studied in purely psychological ways so as to discover the mental processes that underlie the way in which speakers turn propositional messages into the sounds that come from their mouths when they speak (e.g., Levelt, 1989), or the ways in which hearers convert the tiny impulses made by speech sounds impinging on the eardrum into the propositional message the hearer extracts from speech sounds (e.g., Frazier, 1979). However one goes about it, if speaking and hearing are to be understood, then psychological investigation will play an important part.

Speaking and hearing (linguistic performance) can also be studied within a social and cultural framework, with the aim of understanding why and how humans communicate with each other in the ways that they do. Every speaker has a range of communicative competencies that enables him or her to function as a social being. Human linguistic performance cannot be understood without a sociocultural context (Holmes, 1992; Hymes, 1968). A fully adequate theory of speaking must, at least in part, integrate social and psychological theories, because both are significant in explaining how speakers come to speak. This book attempts such an integration.

In addition to the Chomskian sense of the word *performance,* there is a second and more commonly understood sense. This is the sense of performing, for example, in plays, in giving speeches, and in telling stories. Such performances are therefore performances in two senses of the word: The speaker is speaking, that is, involved in activity or behavior, and those who are being spoken to also recognize that there is something special about the way the speaker is speaking, that is, the speech is worthy of the kind of attention people give to performances. To quote Bauman (1986) again on this second sense of performance:

> I understand performance as a mode of communication, a way of speaking, the
> essence of which resides in the assumption of responsibility to an audience for a
> display of communicative skill, highlighting the way in which communication is
> carried out, above and beyond its referential content. From the point of view of the
> audience, the act of expression on the part of the performer is thus laid open to
> evaluation for the way it is done, for the relative skill and effectiveness of the
> performer's display . . . . Viewed in these terms, performance may be understood as
> an enactment of the poetic function, the essence of spoken artistry. (p. 3)

Performances with the properties Bauman described are special partly because they involve factors such as extra effort, practice, and training. They are different from normal speech just as the walking of those who compete at races in the Olympic Games is different from normal walking. It is still walking but it has been modified for particular effects. The performers in this book are notable both because of the way in which they have learned to perform and the special character of their performances. They do not produce great art, but I will suggest that the two kinds of performance—the business of speaking on the one hand and speaking as an enactment of the poetic function on the other hand—often cannot be clearly differentiated in the performances of auctioneers and sportscasters. Their performances allow us, in turn, to explore the character of a larger range of performers whom we can term oral formulaic performers. This exploration will also explain facets—both psychological and sociocultural—of every speaker's speech because we are all, at times, formulaic performers in our normal everyday speech.

I propose, following Pawley and Syder (1983), that part of a speaker's ability to communicate using language has to do with the ability to sound nativelike, that is, to use expressions that other speakers recognize as being the way native speakers of their language say that sort of thing. For example, one greets people in a nativelike way in New Zealand by saying things like *Gidday,* or *How are you?* or *Hi!* One does not say *Are you in good health?* or, as a Chinese speaker might say in similar circumstances, *Have you eaten?* This means that a native speaker must know which expressions are nativelike, and so it follows that they must be in the native speaker's internal dictionary. This internal dictionary contains many lexical items. Some of these are words. Some are idioms. The kinds of lexical items that are linked to social tasks I term *formulae.*

Formulae make the business of speaking (and that of hearing) easier. I assume that when a speaker uses a formula he or she needs only to retrieve it from the dictionary instead of building it up from its constituent parts. In other words, such expressions likely exist as whole or part utterances within the speaker's dictionary and need not be built up from scratch on every new occasion. The facility that this gives speakers Pawley and Syder (1983) termed *nativelike fluency.* The hearer, in turn, also benefits; the hearer needs only to look the expression up in his or her dictionary rather than analyzing the expression as a complex function of its parts.

Because formulae are used to perform social functions, such as to greet people and to apologize, they can provide an insight into the society in which they are used. Their selection is triggered by the speaker's desire to accomplish particular social ends. So when formulae appear in speech, the social factors that led to their being selected are clear to native speakers because such speakers have grown up in the same culture. It follows that the study of formulaic speech has things to tell us about the way in which speech fits into its social and cultural surroundings.

PROBLEMS OF PERFORMANCE

Look again at walking. When human beings walk they stand on one leg after another alternately almost all the time, while simultaneously moving forward. Everything is smoothly integrated and what is going on is not noticed until it malfunctions.

Then we do notice. We notice someone with a neuromuscular disorder walking with great difficulty, thrusting out first one foot and then the other, twisting the torso to get each leg going in the right direction. This is, in its major aspects, just like the walking we all do but it lacks the unconscious ease of natural walking. It lacks fluency.

It is like that with speech. Talkers perform a multiplicity of integrated actions. Some of these involve turning the vocal cords on and off. Others involve moving the tongue to various positions in the mouth. Still others move the soft palate, the lips, and the pharynx. Each set of muscles used in performing these actions is different. Each has motor nerves of different length making the muscles perform while other nerves feed back the actions of the muscles to the brain. That is only the physical part of the performance. In addition, our brains must be coordinating all the activity and giving it meaning and purpose.

How can this complex performance be explained? Clearly there are many factors involved and explanations are unlikely to be simple. This book poses two general questions about performance:

- How do humans speak creatively and yet appropriately in particular situations?
- Given the psychological nature of human memory and processing capacities, how is it that people can keep up speaking at the rate they do without getting behind?

Both problems are not apparent to us as speakers because we do not see anything remarkable about our capacity to speak. After all, almost all humans appear to do it without effort. But not withstanding the fact that we speak with ease, only a moment's reflection will persuade one that this is not a simple matter and that there must be answers to both these questions if we are to understand something of the abilities of smooth talkers.

I will answer these two questions in the light of some traditional answers. The anthropologist Bronislaw Malinowski and the English linguist J. R. Firth provide what looks like an attempt at a solution to the question relating to the appropriateness of speech to its context:

> As sociologists we are not interested in what A or B may feel *qua* individuals, in the accidental course of their own personal experiences—we are interested only in what they feel and think *qua* members of a given community. Now in this capacity, their mental states receive a certain stamp, become stereotyped by the institutions in which they live, by the influence of tradition and folk-lore, by the very vehicle of thought, that is by language. (Malinowski, 1922, p. 23)

> The flesh and blood, the kith and kin, the actual stages of growth in the long process of social incorporation from lying and sleeping, through the sitting up stage, crawling about, walking alone away from home, pre-school freedom, various stages of school, puberty, adolescence, to adult responsibility. For each stage there is a relevant living

space, a relevant culture, a relevant language. The biological individual gradually becomes a bundle of personae, a social personality with many ear languages, one or more hand languages, and one or two tongue languages—a Babel in himself. (Firth, 1964, p. 91)

These two statements stipulate that speech is always socially appropriate because it is always learned in particular nonlinguistic contexts. Consequently it follows that speech is memorized along with its context. Speaking is therefore a matter of recalling speech in the context in which it is appropriate. Neither Malinowski nor Firth had anything to say about the detail of how this works. It is also clearly false for many kinds of utterance, such as an original book of poems.[1] Furthermore, if speech merely involved memorizing verbatim a whole vocabulary of expressions, then it could not be novel. But speech clearly is novel in many cases—new expressions and utterances are produced and old ones adapted to new circumstances.

The following chapters explore a version of these theories about the interrelationship between speech and the situation in which it is learned and spoken, which does not have the consequence of being unable to explain speech novelty. It will do so in detail. I propose that speakers frequently use formulae. Such formulae are learned in specific contexts and are used in those contexts for conventional reasons.

This proposal has a further antecedent, which addresses the second question posed earlier, namely how we are able to speak given our psychological makeup and its limitations. The theory of formulaic speech developed by Milman Parry (1930, 1932) and Albert Lord (1960) is, among other things, an attempt at a solution to the question of how we become able to speak in real time, the time it takes to say what we wish to say. Lord's (1960) theory was designed to explain only the speech of Serbo-Croatian oral poets. He put the solution as follows: "He (the oral poet) is forced by the rapidity of composition in performance to use . . . traditional elements. . . . Yet he practices great freedom in his use of them because they are themselves so flexible" (pp. 4–5). This hypothesis amounts to the following: Because speech such as that of the oral poet is subject to the constraints of real-time performance, the poet does not compose from scratch but uses memorized bits of speech, *traditional elements*. These bits of memorized speech are also flexible. In other words, they permit a degree of novelty.

The studies that have been made within the framework of Parry and Lord's work have depended on the important concept of ritual or routine. We can take it that much of what humans do is done within a context of routine action. For example, my mornings at the bathroom handbasin are, to an extent, routine, that is, rule-governed. There is no particular reason other than habit why I should first put in my contact lenses before shaving because I am nearsighted and can see perfectly well in the bathroom mirror to shave. There is also no practical reason why I should

---

[1]See Langendoen (1968) for an account of the work of Malinowski and Firth.

first put my right lens in and then the left. There is also no reason why I should start shaving on the left side of my face. This is essentially a private routine without any social sanction. Clearly I could, at any time and without any social cost, switch the sequence of some of the operations. Other routines, however, are socially significant. They range from casual greetings to ceremonies that mark rites of passage such as marriage services. They are often just as predictable and just as arbitrary.

Routines often have two significant properties in being both sequentially and hierarchically organized. If we return to my morning routine at the handbasin, the routine is clearly sequential in that one action follows another. I take my lens case and the small rinsing basin from the medicine cabinet, fill the basin with rinsing solution, then take the right lens from the case and rinse it, take it from the solution, place it on my finger and position it on my eyeball, and so forth. However, placing my contact lenses in my eyes is clearly a different routine from shaving. The whole morning routine might be broken down into two higher or macrolevel routines (i.e., shaving, placing contact lenses), each of which in turn can be broken down into component or microroutines. This gives this routine both temporal sequence and hierarchical organization.

My morning routine at the handbasin is not accompanied by speech, but many human routines are accompanied by speech and there are other routines that consist mainly of speech. In the following chapters we will see that sequentially and hierarchically organized routine events are present in a number of dissimilar situations and that they interact with speech in significant ways. As Hymes (1968) put it, "A linguistic routine is a recurrent sequence of verbal behaviour, whether conventional or idiosyncratic" (p. 126).

The terms *routine* and *ritual* are often used interchangeably. I will define *routine* as the more general term. Routines are sequentially and hierarchically organized events in which humans are the active participants. Rituals are those routines that are perceived to have cultural or social significance. In my culture, my morning routines are not culturally significant but a marriage ceremony is. The speech of the performers that is explored in the following chapters takes place in both ritual and routine nonlinguistic contexts. Speech is embedded in these contexts. It is itself routine, that is, sequentially and hierarchically structured. Notwithstanding that, there is still room for novelty. In other words, the speech of auctioneers and sportscasters is significantly like that of the oral poets whose performances were studied by Parry and Lord.

The way we have looked at performance so far allows it to be viewed within three levels of analysis that Bauman (1975) suggested are essential for the study of performance: textual, contextual, and sociocultural. The specific linguistic properties of performances are to be textually studied. This means that there are innumerable linguistic features of performances viewed as texts that might be documented, such as the accent of the speaker, his or her phonology or intonation, or preferred sentence structure. It is a matter of judgment which of these features is significant in coming to understand what makes texts of a specific kind, like, say, auction talk, characteristically different from other kinds of texts.

Contextually each text can be studied by relating it to the immediate situation in which it occurs. All performances are, to a greater or lesser extent, a function of the immediate contexts in which they are produced. For example, there are linguistic features of speech that are characteristically found in lecture halls and not on baseball diamonds.

Finally, texts can also be looked at in terms of their wider significance as social and cultural artifacts. When texts are themselves routines that have cultural significance, or form part of or are accompaniments to other routines that have cultural significance, they are themselves cultural artifacts. For example, the opening utterance of the chair at a meeting consists of a sequence of words, such as *The time is now two o'clock so I will declare the meeting open.*[2] The utterance is a cultural artifact in that such an utterance acts as a meeting opening. No other action is required.

In every case where we will be looking at texts produced by sportscasters and auctioneers I present these by first describing a typical context of occurrence. I will also look at the social and cultural significance these texts have within their respective contexts. Chapter 2 looks at how sports commentators relay the events they see. Such commentary texts are performed in routine contexts because the events that sports commentators describe for their audiences are highly repetitive. On the basis of an analysis of the speech of commentators, I propose that when speakers find themselves having to perform in particular ways, the texts they produce have particular linguistic properties. In this case, rapid time pressures to speak produce increasingly formulaic oral performances. Chapter 3 tests this theory by looking at the texts produced by auctioneers, another group of speakers under considerable speaking pressure. The analysis there indicates that the predictive theory proposed in chapter 2 is supported. Chapter 4 investigates the way the formulaic linguistic resources that smooth talkers—both sportscasters and auctioneers—draw on come into existence and how smooth talkers acquire them. The goal of the last chapter is to offer specific answers to the two questions posed earlier and prefigured in the work of Malinowski, Firth, Parry, and Lord, namely how speakers come to speak in real time, appropriately, yet with novel utterances. The explanation is that many speakers incorporate characteristics of smooth talking, specifically the use of traditional formulae, into their ordinary speech and thus speak fluently and appropriately in routine contexts.

The texts for these analyses were collected over 18 years in a variety of English-speaking countries: New Zealand, the United States, Canada, and England. They came to be collected in part by accident. As a graduate student in Canada, I became fascinated by ice hockey and the capacity of its commentators to keep up

---

[2]If I am directly quoting from an utterance I have recorded, I use quotation marks. In all other instances where I use a cited form as an example it is in italics.

with the game. Later, I happened to be at a livestock auction collecting samples of spontaneous conversation and heard auctioneers performing rapidly in ways that struck me as fascinating. Since then, I have attended auctions in other parts of the world to see if there are common features of auction speech, and later to test the theory that auction speech in part results from speakers having to perform at speed in real time. I have transcribed only a small proportion of the total number of performances that form the empirical domain of this study. The business of transcribing speech is hugely time consuming and, after a certain amount of text is transcribed, pointless, because the next text tells one little if anything that one does not already know.

The majority of the texts that form the corpus of transcripts on which the theories to follow are based were recorded in Christchurch, New Zealand. One reason for this is that acquiring something like a nativelike understanding of context is required to analyze any text for its communicative import. I am close enough to being a native of Christchurch. The other is the practical matter of having at hand any number of appropriate speakers who are willing to be recorded. I know that texts with the linguistic features of these texts can be collected in many other places by those who are native to those places. I am presuming, in other words, that there is nothing exotic in these texts coming from an island in the southern hemisphere and that speech of the same essential kind may be found in many settings.

2

The Speech of Sports Commentators

COMMENTARIES

The sports about which the commentators in this chapter give instant accounts are either fast moving, making it particularly difficult for commentators to be fluent, or slow moving, making it difficult for the commentator to fill in the time with talk. These speed factors can be assumed to create psychological problems for the speaker and the solution of those problems must be answered in psychological terms. In more detail the problems come about as follows. Fast sports make talk difficult because the faster the sport, the more difficult it will be for the commentator to provide an instantaneous commentary on it. The task of a commentator describing a fast sport is like that of simultaneous translators who must say in one language what they hear in another without getting left behind, that is, they must translate in real time (Yaghi, 1994). The problem of translating in real time can be stated quite simply; it is that the lag between the time the translator hears something in one language and the time they say it in the other must be short and must not get longer. This is because humans cannot commit large amounts of text to memory at the same time as speaking the translation of something they heard a few minutes ago.

The commentator of a fast sport is in a similar position, except that what the commentator of a fast sport says must be translated from a visual input rather than an auditory one. The commentator must also not get behind. If he or she does, then there will be more and more of the game that has elapsed and must be remembered in order for it to be recounted. There will come a point, in that case, where omission is inevitable because people can only recall so much from memory.

The commentator of a slow sport has a different problem: how to keep talking while little of note is happening. This is not a problem that has to do with memory because there is little to recall. Instead, it has to do with filling the time between notable events with talk.

In looking at these two speech tasks I am addressing the problem raised in chapter 1 of how speakers are able to speak in real time.

RACE CALLING[1]

Our first texts are taken from the speech of race callers. The discussion of race calling is based on that of New Zealand race callers, particularly Reon Murtha who is the local caller in Christchurch. My research associates and I have also listened to commentaries from many other New Zealand callers and samples of Australian, British, and one U. S. caller. Race callers are chosen because they relay events that take place at speed. In order to understand these texts we first look at the context in which they occur.

Routine Events

The chant of the horserace caller is a familiar sound in suburbia on weekends in both Australia and New Zealand. Coming over the airwaves and emitting from transistor radios, it mingles with the sound of lawnmowers and alternates with the more tranquil tones of the cricket commentator.

Horse races proceed in a particularly obvious fashion. The horses line up at the start of the course. In the case of galloping races, the horses are confined in cages and the front door to the cage is opened at the start. In the case of trotting and pacing races, the horses may be lined up at a standing start or at a mobile start. After the start, the field of runners makes one or more circuits of the track before passing the finishing post. (For an ethnographic account of horse racing see Harrah, 1992.)

The commentator's speech task is to indicate the order of the runners as they go through this apparently simple process. To do this, the race caller stands in a high location with his binoculars on a supporting rail, a lip microphone in front of his mouth. Lip microphones pick up very little sound unless it is made very close to the microphone. Before the start, the caller can take note of salient facts about some or all of the horses, sometimes noting the number and driver, or rider, the trainer, and perhaps the owner(s). A caller might note the starting place of the horse, or details about individual idiosyncrasies in starts, such as the behavior of unruly, difficult, or good starters. Then there are the gambling odds associated with the race, the favorites for the race and what they and all the runners are currently paying. Because the activity before the start is leisurely, at this stage a commentator always relates events in *color commentary mode*. The term *color commentary* is taken from the operation of commentary pairs in many sports where one commentator calls the play-by-play and the other provides comments when the game is interrupted. Such pairs exist in the commentary of ice hockey, basketball, cricket, football, and no doubt many other sports. The two kinds of commentary have different linguistic properties, as we shall see. (See also Ferguson, 1983.)

The commentary in *play-by-play mode* begins at the start of the race proper. The start of the race is almost always signaled by a single verbal formula such as *Racing*

---

[1] An earlier version of this section was published as Kuiper and Austin (1990). For a comparative account of the speech of another fast sport, ice hockey, see Kuiper and Haggo (1985).

now. At that point, the on-course public address system switches the commentator's voice on for the on-course patrons. There are idiosyncratic variations in the exact time of the switch from color into play-by-play mode. Some commentators take a few seconds to switch from color to play-by-play mode; others switch into play-by-play mode at the moment the race commences. In the following commentary the color opening runs from Line I.1 to I.15. The closing color section is from Lines I.109 to I.153.

Discourse Structure of Play-by-Play Race Calling

The race commentary indicates the position of the runners, starting at the leading horse and ending with the horse at the tail of the field. That is its main communicative function. This can be called a *cycle.* In the following commentary, there are nine cycles.

The following sample text is taken from a race meeting where it was the fourth race of the day ("the fourth race on the card"). The race took place at the Addington Raceway in Christchurch, New Zealand, which is used for harness racing. The start for this race is a mobile start in which the horses line up behind a barrier on the back of a vehicle. The vehicle picks up speed, the horses behind follow and as the vehicle and the following horses approach the start, the barrier folds away and the vehicle speeds up and moves out of the way of the horses. The company that manufactures Lion Brown, a New Zealand beer, is the sponsor for this race. The race is 2,000 meters long and for 3-year-olds. The commentator is Reon Murtha. This commentary is not included here because it is particularly unusual but because it is normal. It was recorded off air on October 15, 1986.[2]

I.1	This is the first heat of the Lion Brown Rising Star
	3-Year-Old championships and the first four that
	are placed in this qualify for the grand final here in
	just a week, Friday week. Thirty thousand dollar race,
I.5	the final. The favorite is number five, Race Ruler,
	although you wouldn't think it if the dividends on the
	board are anything to go by. At the moment it's paying
	eleven dollars but that's not quite true. It was two
	dollars before and I just think something's wrong with
I.10	those dividends that are showing up on our screen.
	They've got Speedy Cheval the favorite but I'm not
	exactly sure that that's correct but anyway they're in
	behind the mobile going towards the starting point now
	for the first heat of the Lion Brown Rising Star 3-
I.15	Year-Old Championship just about there.

---

[2]Transcripts are numbered sequentially with roman numerals within each chapter, and the lines within each transcript are numbered in fives in the left-hand margin with a period between the transcript and line numbers.

They're off and racing now.
And one of the best out was Speedy Cheval
coming out at number two from El Red
and also Florlis Fella's away fairly well
I.20   a little wider on the track the favorite Race Ruler.
Twilight Time is in behind those.
Breaking up behind is Noodlum's Fella
and he went down
and one tipped out was My Dalrae
I.25   and the driver's out of the sulkie.
The horse actually went down on its nose and cartwheeled,
sulkie over the top.
They race their way down the far side
1600 to go
I.30   and El Red stoked up to go to the lead now.
Race Ruler's going to be caught without cover
followed by Speedy Cheval in the trail.
Florlis Fella was next
followed then by Twilight Time.
I.35   Little River's got a nice passage through over on the outside.
Megatrend next along the rail
followed then by Lone Eagle.
About two lengths away is Belvedere.
Belvedere was followed by False Image
I.40   and one buried on the inside of those two was Catarina.
But they race through the straight in a bunch now
with 1300 meters left to go.
El Red the leader by two lengths from Speedy Cheval
the favorite Race Ruler parked on the outside
I.45   followed by Florlis Fella.
Twilight Time's up against the rail.
Megatrend the inside is joined on the outside by Little River.
Lone Eagle and Catarina were next.
They were followed then by Belvedere
I.50   and last of all would have been False Image.
They race their way around the showgrounds bend into the back
1100 meters to go
and El Red the leader by two lengths
from Speedy Cheval and Race Ruler.
I.55   On the rails to Twilight Time.
Belvedere is going up three wide.
Florlis Fella in the center.
False Image attacking around three wide.
In between them is Little River.
I.60   Lone Eagle is up three wide

and Megatrend
and Catarina.
Down to the 800 meters goes El Red the leader.
It's El Red in front now
I.65   being joined by Belvedere half a length away.
Race Ruler right in behind them.
Speedy Cheval's up against the rail.
They were followed by False Image getting closer.
Twilight Time on the inside of Florlis Fella.
I.70   Then Little River.
Lone Eagle around those pretty wide
and back behind them Megatrend and Catarina.
They travel off the back
500 meters to run
I.75   and the big chestnut El Red by half a length the leader.
They're attacking him now though
and False Image has gone round in a couple of strides
to take the lead.
It's False Image from El Red
I.80   and Belvedere
and Race Ruler
and Florlis Fella is about four wide.
Speedy Cheval is locked up in the inside
and further out to Little River.
I.85   They turn for home.
240 to go.
False Image scampers clear by a couple of lengths.
Here's Florlis Fella unwinding
and through the middle Race Ruler.
I.90   He's coming home great guns.
Up the center then Little River
and Catarina's flying home
too late perhaps.
False Image.
I.95   But Race Ruler's got to him.
Race Ruler in front now
from Florlis Fella and False Image.
False Image will hold second down to the post.
Race Ruler won it.
I.100   False Image followed by Florlis Fella,
Catarina.
Then Megatrend.
It was followed home over on the inside of those by Little River.
Then Twilight Time,
I.105   Belvedere,

Speedy Cheval,

El Red,

and Lone Eagle.

And the other one that didn't complete the journey or

I.110   two of them: Noodlum's Fella was one, and the other one
over on the far side of the course ah also catapulted
and let's have a look to see how he is, number seven
over there, My Dalrae. What a spectacular spill. He
actually decided to, once he got loose from his

I.115   driver, he bounded away by himself. The sulkie was on
its side and just as the sulkie tipped over on its
wheels ah he missed his footing ah he went into a
break, tripped, fell, went down on his nose, and then
absolutely catapulted with the sulkie right over on top

I.120   of him and ah he's back on his feet so luckily, I
suppose, he's come away with a few abrasions but it the
horse looks as though he is walking OK so he hasn't
done any serious damage to himself and the driver is
quite OK, Tony Robb, My Dalrae. Noodlum's Fella was the

I.125   one that broke. He ah this sort of thing happened to
him on Saturday out at Banks Peninsula when he was
another, he was one who came down in that race. So two
in a row.

Here's the call, Number five the winner. Good

I.130   performance. Five. So five, nine, four, thirteen, the
judge's call. A close photo for fourth. Number five,
Race Ruler, the winner and Race Ruler I can give you
all the details now. He's paid a dollar ninety and a
dollar thirty. A dollar ninety and a dollar thirty.

I.135   Number nine is second. False Image has paid four
dollars twenty five. And the third one to pass, number
four, Florlis Fella, who paid two dollars fifty, a
dollar ninety. A dollar thirty, four dollars twenty
five, two dollars fifty. The quinella, seventeen

I.140   dollars forty five. Seventeen forty five. The
trifecta, two hundred and forty six dollars. Two forty
six dollars, the trifecta and the double on races three
and four, one, Bronze Tiger and number five, Race
Ruler, sixty nine dollars seventy. Sixty nine dollars

I.145   seventy. And the concession, seventy nine dollars
sixty five. Seventy nine sixty five.

He's a good horse, Race Ruler. He's proved that he's
possibly the best three year old in the country at the
moment and was one of the top 2-year-olds last year.

I.150   Didn't ah start in all of the classics because he

wasn't ah entered for them. But won the major ones ah
and ah he's certainly a very fine looking 3-year-
old this season.

This transcript shows that for each cycle, horses are described as being closest
to the rail or further out or behind other horses. This kind of description continues
until the last horse is reached, after which the commentator loops back to the head
of the field, often using a standard expression, such as *they pass the 100-meter mark.*
A *loop,* as well as getting the caller from the tail of the field back to the front runners
at the head of the field, also tells the audience two things: that the cycle is about to
begin again and where in the race the leading horses are currently. This latter end
is accomplished by indicating the location of the field in the race and on the course.
The loops in the commentary transcript are at Lines I.28–29, I.41–42, I.51–52, I.63,
I.73–74, and I.85–86.

Near the end of the race, the cycles are often incomplete in that the whole field
is not covered. The cycle then becomes a naming of the leading contenders, often
without clear locations for them being specified. After the horses pass the finishing
post there is a last pass through the whole cycle, toward the end of which the
commentator moves from play-by-play mode back into color mode. In the
preceding commentary the prefinish cycles, in which the whole field is not covered,
begin at Line I.75.

After completion of that cycle, the commentator switches to color description
of various further features of the race, such as whether a photo has been called.
Photos are called when the finish is particularly close. The judges then use the photo
of the finishing post at the time the first horses pass it to separate the place getters.
The final section of commentary often includes the gambling consequences of the
final placings. The on-course public address system relaying the commentary is
switched off during this color commentary epilogue.

A set of idealized discourse structure rules for the play-by-play commentary can
be given as in Fig. 2.1.[3]

Each rule specifies the sequential structure of part of the race. The first rule
specifies the structure of the whole race, namely that it consists of a number of
cycles, each followed by a loop ending in the finish of the race and a final cycle.
Rule 2 specifies the internal structure of each cycle and Rule 3 the structure of the
loop.

There are idiosyncrasies among race callers in the way they use this set of rules.
For example, in the middle phase of the race, some callers call every horse whereas
others call only the leading contenders. Lachie Marshall, who calls races in Oamaru

---

[3]These rules can be understood as instructions for drawing tree diagram representations where the
left-hand item before the arrow is the category on top of the tree or subtree and the right-hand elements
are the structural units that are dominated by the left-hand unit. Parentheses around a constituent indicate
that it is optional. Braces indicate that the constituents enclosed by the braces are alternatives. Formally
these are context-free rewrite rules and rules such as these can be used to define any linear sequence
that has hierarchical organization.

R1 Racing ---> (pre-start) + start + 1st cycle + loop + 2nd cycle + loop + ... + finish +
     final cycle

R2 Cycle ----> location of xth horse in field + $\left(\left\{ \begin{array}{l} \text{untoward happening} \\ \text{field locator} \end{array} \right\} \right)$
     where x ranges in sequence from the first horse through to the last horse
     in the field.

R3 Loop ----> (track location) + (field location)

() represent optional constituents
{} represent alternative constituents.

FIG. 2.1. Discourse structure rules for racing commentaries in play-by-play mode.

in the southern half of the South Island of New Zealand, runs through the leaders again in a short cycle if he has just called the leaders and found there to be a change. He then goes on to give the whole field. In the prefinish phase of the commentary the number of horses covered and the number of cycles varies from caller to caller. Reon Murtha from Christchurch covers about six horses out of, say, 10 or 15, and cycles only a few times with a reduced field. In discussion with me he explained that all of the horses have someone betting on them so everyone has a right to hear how their horse is doing until the last possible moment when only a few horses still have some chance of being "in the money," that is, able to pay a dividend. Allan Bright from Wellington, on the other hand, covers between three and six horses in the prefinish phase and may relate the order of the front runners half a dozen times.

Formulae of Race Calling

In addition to the speech of race callers being organized according to discourse structure rules, it is also made up of formulae. A formula has the following linguistic properties:

1. It is a lexical item consisting of a sequence of words.
2. It has syntactic structure.
3. It has specific conditions of use, that is, it does particular work for a speaker in a given situation.

(We look at each of these properties in greater detail later.)

It follows from the fact that formulae are lexical items that they are psychological units because lexical items are stored in a speaker's memory. The evidence for supposing something to be a formula must often be gained by studying its frequency of occurrence in speech or in texts, as scholars of oral literature tend to do, but observation of frequency is not the sole way of testing for whether an expression is a formula. Psychological tests may also be employed. For example, speakers who know a formula will be able to finish it once they recognize its beginning. The very fact that native speakers recognize an expression as a formula can be used to identify formulae.

Like all lexical items, formulae show both an arbitrariness of form and idiosyncrasy of behavior. The arbitrariness of form exhibits itself in the fact that although some formulae have variant forms, there are many other ways of saying the same thing that a native speaker would not use. For example, the formulae Reon Murtha uses when race calling include the loop formula "round the showgrounds bend they come" but not *round the showgrounds bend they trot.* This latter expression is used by no caller my students and I have recorded and I would predict that anyone familiar with race calling would know that this is not the way to indicate the location of the field on the Addington track. The former expression is therefore Murtha's preferred and only way of relating the fact that the field of runners is at that particular section of the track. It is presumably held in and recalled from Murtha's memory; otherwise it would not come out the same way every time. It is a well-formed syntactic structure and thus has all the properties required for an expression to be a formula.

The play-by-play section of the preceding text has a formula on every line. The evidence for this is contained in a dictionary built up from transcriptions of a sample of over 50 races, where formulae were placed on cards and compared for their reappearance in other commentaries and for their familiarity to one consultant linguist whose family owned and followed race horses. This dictionary is constructed according to where each formula operates in the discourse structure of the commentary. Here is a small selection of formulae from the dictionary arranged in such a way. Formulae used in the preceding transcript are indicated in parentheses.

1. Start formula:
   a. There they go.
   b. They're away and racing.
   c. They're off and racing now.   (I.16)
   d. They're on their way.
2. Locator formulae:
   a. threading its way through
   b. caught without cover   (I.31)
   c. settling back a little bit
   d. getting through on the inside
   e. at the tail end of the field
   f. going around them
3. Loop formulae:
   a. They pass the judge.
   b. Round the turn they come.
   c. Into the straight they come.
   d. They turn for home.   (I.85)
   e. Out of the straight for the first time.

4. Win formulae:
   a. They go to the post.
   b. X has won it.   (I.99)
   c. X got it won.

Fluency

The problems of providing a contemporaneous commentary of a fast sport put a premium on fluency. If the speaker can keep up a steady flow of speech, then he can stick with the events as they unfold and not get behind the action. A commentator, unlike the horses he is describing, cannot break down by ceasing to speak, being extremely disfluent and the like, because the commentator is providing live radio commentary. Therefore, as noted earlier, fluency is essential. But, as also noted earlier, horse racing commentaries are in two modes: the play-by-play and color mode. It is only during the play-by-play section that fluency is essential. It is also here that one would think it the most difficult to maintain. Before the race little is happening and speech is in color mode. At the end of a race, after the horses have passed the winning post, the action, insofar as it matters, is also over. So the caller's speech can revert to a more normal mode. When it does, disfluencies of the normal kind occur. Hesitations increase, as illustrated in the epilogue of the sample text given earlier. There are a number of voiced pauses, for example, ah. The syntax becomes disfluent as well, as the two false starts in the epilogue section of the sample text show: "He actually decided to, once he'd got loose from his driver, he bounded away by himself" (I.113–115). "He ah this sort of thing happened . . ." (I.125).

This can be contrasted with an example from a different commentary in which disfluency is apparently masked during a play-by-play section. In this example, there are no hesitations and two formulae are juxtaposed while the commentator searches for the correct name of a horse: "They were followed through there now by as they make their way on to the top end of the course by Bahrein." The formula that is interrupted is *They were followed through there now by X,* where X is the name of a horse. The formula that seamlessly (i.e., without hesitation such as pausing) follows on is *As they make their way on to the top end of the course.* This formula is a field locator formula, that is, one that locates the field of runners in the race or on the track, rather than a horse locator formula that locates an individual horse relative to another. We can surmise that Reon Murtha is having a problem retaining fluency, the probable cause being either that he cannot immediately recall the name of the horse he is looking at or that he cannot pick out which horse is next because it is masked in some way, for instance by another horse. The evidence for this comes from his selection of formulae. Murtha normally uses formulae that locate the whole field of runners only when looping back to commence another cycle. Yet here there is such a formula interpolated into a horse locator formula. This is most likely designed to create a short period of time during which he can find the horse's name, either by recognizing it through the binoculars or by recalling its name from memory. The use of the formula clearly enables him to remain fluent. The fluency of the entire play-by-play sections of commentary is manifested in lack of pausing, both voiced and unvoiced, and the very regular syllable-per-second delivery rate. Therefore, it seems that fluency is able to be maintained through stringing together one formula after another.

Droned or Chanted Intonation

Racing commentaries in play-by-play mode are droned or chanted, that is, they are basically articulated in a monotone. The intonational note usually rises in semitones to a high point at the finishing post and then gradually comes down as the commentator moves through the last cycle. On the way down the commentator also moves out of this mode back into color mode with normal speech intonation. If we time the movement up the scale as the race proceeds, then at the beginning of the race the semitone steps up at about 30-second intervals between which the caller's voice stays on one note. As the race proceeds these intervals get shorter and shorter until right at the end only a few seconds separate each step up. At this stage some commentators move stepwise, whereas others move on a sliding scale, so that one cannot tell exactly on which syllable the rise in pitch takes place. After the horses have passed the winning post the commentator slides all the way down the scale again and ends up speaking normally.

Although this is a description of the archetypal intonation pattern there are variations. If a particularly exciting event takes place there will be a larger jump. In the sample text, this takes place at the point at which one of the drivers is pitched out of the sulkie (the two-wheeled carts from which drivers in harness races drive the horses), beginning at Line I.22. At that point the caller jumps up three semitones. However, Reon Murtha's commentaries always span an octave from the start to the winning post. The normal accelerating stepwise rise in pitch has, in this case, been interrupted by a much larger than normal step up. So for the remaining part of the commentary, Murtha lengthens the time between steps up the scale until he is again at the point he would normally be and then goes through the rapid rises in pitch that normally accompany the last few hundred meters of the race. This intonational melody and a more typical one for comparison are shown in Fig. 2.2.

There are a number of variations among callers in the way they perform. In a drone, a speaker consistently speaks in a monotone with little or no normal speech intonation (although a drone may be accompanied by various kinds of ornamentation, as discussed later). Drones may also be chanted. Chant is what happens when drone is sung. Drone is therefore a kind of speech and chant is a kind of singing. What drone and chant share is a strong tonal center, rather like the pedal base in baroque music, with some room for ornamentation. Some race callers chant and some drone. Reon Murtha, Lachie Marshall from Oamaru, and Dave McDonald from Gore all chant, whereas Keith Haub from Auckland drones.

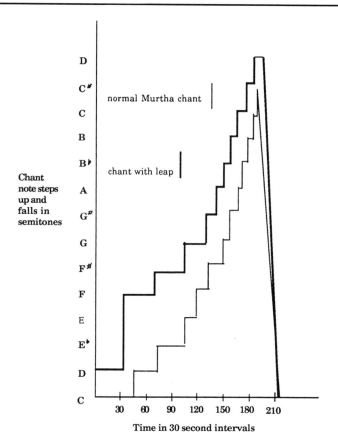

FIG. 2.2. Two chants of Reon Murtha showing the stepwise rises in pitch over time.

Whether one drones or chants appears to be, in part, a matter of tradition. For example, Reon Murtha says that Keith Haub from Auckland has modeled himself on the call of Bill Collins who calls races in Melbourne, Australia. It seems, on listening to both of them, that there is a close resemblance in their calling styles. Those callers who follow in the tradition of the great Dave Clarkson, such as Reon Murtha and Peter Kelly, chant because Dave Clarkson chanted. Reon Murtha told me that he modeled himself on Dave Clarkson and that Clarkson is regarded by many callers on the South Island and the southern part of the North Island of New Zealand as their model.

A second way callers vary their drone is in their pitch range, which tends to be unique for any particular commentator. Reon Murtha typically covers one complete octave from D to D while calling a single race. This is shown in Fig. 2.2. Keith Haub in one race had a much smaller range of $C^{\#}$ to G.

Commentators also have intonational ornaments of various kinds. For example, Reon Murtha uses a fall tune, that is, a slight drop in pitch on the last stressed syllable of formulae which are in turn at the end of particular sections of the discourse, for example, at the completion of a cycle. This is not invariably the case. He might produce six fall tunes in a race where four come at cycle boundaries and two do not. In another it might be two at cycle boundaries and two at random. In contrast, Dave McDonald on occasion drops a half tone on the first syllable of a formula before returning to the base tone. He also has a very regular fall tune at the end of a cycle.

Conclusion

The linguistic properties of the speech of race callers are as follows: Their discourse is governed closely by sequencing rules, and consists largely of formulae. It is spoken with abnormal fluency, and droned or chanted intonation. Speech with these properties will from now on be called *formulaic speech*. It is my contention that race callers (and other speakers still to pass through the pages of this book) are oral formulaic performers like the Serbo-Croatian poets who were the focus of Parry and Lord's work (see chap. 1). I suggest this because virtually all the main linguistic properties of the songs composed by the oral poets Parry and Lord studied are found in the speech of race callers. Those songs are chanted, they have fixed discourse segments with hierarchical organization, and they are formulaic.

It is possible that the features of formulaic speech thus far described are accidental. This would mean that oral formulaic speech really has no integrity and that its properties are a chance combination of features. It could also be that they are more generally features of spoken unscripted sports commentaries because race calls are indeed unscripted commentaries.[4] That would mean that the features have come together because of the nature of providing commentaries. This second possibility can be investigated by looking at unscripted commentaries of slow events. That is undertaken in the next section of this chapter. The third and more interesting possibility is that a more general explanation exists for the appearance of this cluster of features in the commentaries of fast sports. Supporting the theory of a cognitive and contextual influence on formulaic speech is the burden of chapter 3.

THE LANGUAGE OF UNSCRIPTED COMMENTARY

The general linguistic features of unscripted commentary were investigated by Crystal and Davy (1969) and their account can be drawn on to see if the features of their commentaries and those of race callers are the same. In doing so we move

---

[4]Ferguson (1983) pointed out that the term *commentary* is used in British English for what is termed *announcing* in North American English.

geographically from New Zealand to England. However, it may be supposed that the properties of unscripted commentaries will not be greatly different in the two locations because both have English traditions of radio broadcasting.

Routine Context

The two examples Crystal and Davy used to illustrate their account are commentaries of a cricket match and a parade for a state funeral, both in England. I use the cricket commentary as an illustration. The samples were radio commentaries because on radio the commentator "must recreate for his hearers a chain of activity as it is developing" (Crystal & Davy, 1969, p. 126). This then is no different from the task of the race caller. Cricket like horse races is a routine activity. In a cricket match the same things happen over and over again. A bowler runs in to bowl the ball. A batsman either hits the ball or leaves it alone. If he or she hits the ball, it goes to some location on the field and is picked up by a fielder and returned to the wicketkeeper. If the ball is left alone by the batsman it is stopped by the wicketkeeper. Each kind of hitting, catching, and throwing is itself an instance of a general category. There are hits called *cuts, drives, hooks,* and so forth.

Discourse Structure

Let us suppose that extended sections of speech are planned. This planning must take place at a macrolevel to gain the overall structure the speaker seeks and at a microlevel to provide the desired sequences of sentences, phrases, and words. Cricket commentaries are at times given macro structure through the use of discourse structure rules that determine the order in which things are said. Look, for example, at the central routine activity in cricket, the bowler bowling and the batsman batting.

Here are all the examples contained in Crystal and Davy's (1969, pp. 126–128) sample text.

II.1   McKenzie comes in
       bowls
       and Barrington makes a most ungraceful little jab there
       to a ball that goes through to Grout.

III.1 McKenzie scrubs it furiously on his flannels and starts
       off on that rather buoyant bouncing run of his
       bowls
       and Barrington plays very precisely forward this time.

III.5 His foot is right down the line and he pushes back down
       to the bowler.

IV.1   McKenzie moves in
       bowls

> and Barrington pulling his bat away takes that high on
> the thigh and it pops out to short leg.

V.1   Up again comes McKenzie
        bowls
        And Barrington edges that and it's through the slips
        and he's going to get four runs and a life.

The discourse structure rule organizing these utterances is that the commentator describes the bowler coming in. He then says *bowls* and thereafter describes what happens to the ball after it has reached or passed the batsman. But this is not so much a discourse structure rule as the rule of the bowling routine itself. It is also not the only discourse rule used in cricket commentaries. Pawley (1991) showed that there are various activities in a cricket match that a commentator will relate in similar ways, for instance, score summaries in which the commentator gives the current score in the game. As with many discourse structure rules there are both optional and obligatory sections. Pawley showed that reporting the approach and/or delivery of the ball is obligatory, as Crystal and Davy's examples suggest, and so is the immediate consequence of the ball having been bowled. At that point the batsman has either played a stroke, left the ball alone, been bowled out, and so forth. Whichever event occurs must also be relayed. The relaying of other events, for example, whether a fielder happens to be signing autographs on the edge of the field of play or whether the batsman is wearing a helmet, is optional.

Formulae

There are certainly formulae in the commentaries that Crystal and Davy used as examples. In fact, a good proportion of the cricket commentary consists of formulae. For instance, the one word formula at the center of the bowling routine is always *bowls*. Here is a partial dictionary of some cricket formulae taken from Pawley (1991) and from my own observations.

1. Preinnings formulae:
    a. (team) X won the toss and elected to bat.
    b. (team) X won the toss and put (team) Y in.
2. Predelivery formulae:
    a. (batsman) A is on strike.
3. Delivery formulae:
    a. (bowler) X starts his runup.
    b. (bowler) X comes/runs in.
    c. bowls.
    d. (the delivery) just short of a length.
4. Batsman's response formulae:
    a. (batsman) X comes/moves down the pitch.

b. (batsman) X is beaten in the air.
c. (batsman) X is beaten off the pitch.
d. (batsman) X drives into the covers.
e. the ball goes through to (keeper) X.
5. Score summary formulae:
a. The score goes up to (numeral) X for (numeral) Y
b. (team) X now on (numeral) Y for (numeral) Z.

There are numerous other episodes in a game of cricket that have associated formulae, but unlike race calling, not all the commentary is made up of formulae. For example, the cricket commentator in Crystal and Davy's transcript says at one point "the ball now seems to be coming up on its way to the wicket keeper instead of almost clinging to the ground as it did on Saturday." Because this sentence is not constructed from formulae that have been heard on other occasions and because it is specifically related to an abnormal happening, it seems to be a novel utterance produced for the occasion.

It seems that, as far as their use of discourse structure rules and formulae are concerned, these commentaries are in color mode rather than in the kind of rigid play-by-play mode we saw in race calling. This is because not everything that is said by cricket commentators is structured by discourse structure rules and not all of what is said is said in formulae. One of the color commentators who visits New Zealand from time to time is particularly interested in any seagulls that may sometimes be found at a cricket ground. He often spends time describing what the seagulls are doing and how they impress him by their behavior. For such interludes, there is no prescribed discourse structure and the gentleman who is so taken by seagulls has no specific cricket formulae or even seagull formulae for these often lengthy pieces of discourse that he interpolates into his commentary when the game slows to the point of allowing him to do so.

In summary, it would seem that unscripted commentaries in general and those of the race caller in particular are not categorically different in their use of discourse structure rules and formulae. It is rather a matter of the degree to which they are present. This suggests that any commentary genre can be assessed as to how tightly the discourse is structured by rules and how much of what is said is formulaic. The generalization I propose from the preceding analysis is that in the unscripted commentaries of slow sports like cricket (and I would predict baseball), both discourse structure rules and formulae are likely to be less in evidence than they are in the commentaries of fast sports such as horse racing and ice hockey.

Abnormal Fluency

Crystal and Davy (1969) had this to say about the fluency of the commentators whose speech they describe: "Successful commentary is marked by a fluency far in excess of that found in most other forms of unscripted speech" (p. 130). This fluency is demonstrated through "the complete absence of voiced hesitations," and intonation being used "to connect separate items of information into quite lengthy, coherent sequences" (p. 131). There are additional features of their sample commentaries demonstrating fluency that they do not mention. The commentaries have few false starts and filler words. There is no evidence of self-repair. But they do not have the even articulation rate that was a feature of the speech of race callers and cricket commentaries do contain quite lengthy unvoiced pauses.

Droned Intonation

The commentators of cricket and other slow sports do not speak in a monotone. In fact, as Crystal and Davy pointed out, the commentators try to sound interesting; one way this is done is with variations in intonation and other features of prosodics. For the cricket commentary, "many of the tone-units show highly varied patterns of pitch movement" (Crystal & Davy, 1969, p. 132).

Summary of the Speech of the Commentators of Slow Sports

In the speech of the commentators of slow sports, some episodes of the discourse are tightly rule governed and when they are, formulae are also present; however, these features are not as pervasive as they are in the commentary speech of fast sports. Slow sports commentators are fluent, but their speech does contain pauses and does not have an even articulation rate as measured in syllables per second. The commentators of slow sports do not drone or chant.

CONTRASTS BETWEEN THE COMMENTARIES OF RACING AND OTHER COMMENTARIES

We can draw the following conclusions about the general features of the speech of commentators. First, commentary speech can take place in routine contexts and when it does, its discourse structure always follows the events the commentator is describing in some fashion. It can do this in a tightly organized way through having the whole of what is said organized by discourse structure rules or only sections of it organized this way.

Second, the more narrowly linguistic features may vary within limits. Commentators appear to be abnormally fluent, but the areas in which they are fluent vary. Race callers during the play-by-play section of the race show the most striking fluency with their even rate of articulation, total absence of hesitation, and minimal pausing. In contrast, the cricket commentator pauses rather more often.

The commentaries we have looked at use formulae to some extent. Race commentaries consist almost entirely of formulae, commentators leaving their well-worn ruts only when something unusual happens and then they switch into color mode. However, even in color mode, formulae may be used from time to time when what is being spoken about is a normal event. Cricket commentators use formulae for some of the time in much the same way as race commentators do during the color parts of their performance. Only race callers drone or chant. The commentators of slower sports use a greater repertoire of intonation and pitch range features.

The conclusion to be reached by this contrast is that the cluster of properties that define formulaic speech, namely pervasive use of discourse structure rules and formulae, droned or chanted intonation, and extreme fluency, do not appear in all unscripted commentaries but only the commentaries of fast sports.

FORMULAIC SPEECH AND PROCESSING PRESSURES

Overview

The speech of commentators, it seems, can vary in a number of respects. The events commentators describe are more or less turned into routines and the way they describe them is also turned into routines. One would think that these two factors are related; that is, the more the events themselves are routines, the more routine their commentary must be. This is not entirely the case. Creating routines through the coding of events into discourse structure rules and formulae depends rather more on the speed at which the events themselves proceed and consequently the speed at which the commentator is obliged to process the events he sees, than it does on the routine nature of the external events the commentator is describing. A great deal of what goes on in a cricket game is routine but much of it does not, as we have seen, need to be described in formulaic ways. It happens so slowly that the commentator has time to work out relatively original ways of describing the events he sees. So the speed of external events appears to determine the relative presence of the whole cluster of linguistic properties of commentary speech. The faster the external events and therefore the greater the commentator's obligation to relay them rapidly, the more tightly clustered will be the linguistic features of formulaic speech.

This amounts to an embryonic theory about the nature of formulaic speech. The theory is that using the linguistic resources of formulaic speech is a response by speakers to particular pressures on them. If they must speak fluently and fast when there is also a lot going on outside to which they must attend, then they will resort to using formulaic speech. This is a causal theory that predicts that when specific psychological factors act on speakers, then their speech will have the properties of formulaic speech as already described.

Routine Contexts and Discourse Structure Rules

A sports commentary must follow the game. "A commentary is a spoken account of events which are actually taking place, given for the benefit of listeners who cannot see them" (Crystal & Davy, 1969, p. 125). Insofar as this is so, its discourse structure is externally driven, being dependent on the events the commentator sees. However, it is not just a function of external events. It is also conventionally ordered, because in many situations there are potentially a number of different ways of sequencing the description of the events, yet only one or two of those ways are adopted for a commentary. So the events themselves and the way they are related must map onto one another and this derives from convention.

Commentaries represent the game as it is perceived through an abstract and conventional representation, rather than through its physical manifestation. That is why there is a commentary. If a game were just the visual spectacle and its sound effects, then television, for instance, could present the game almost as the fans in the stands see and hear it. But the camera is selective, showing what seems significant, and the commentator is similarly selective. Not everything that happens on the track is significant; specifically, given our earlier distinction between routine and ritual, not everything is culturally significant. The play-by-play commentator is there to relate the cultural significance of the race. This involves matters having not just to do with the fact that horses are galloping or trotting around a track, as any horse might for recreational purposes. It involves the cultural artifact of this being a race with all that involves, such as competition and resulting winners and losers. In the case of horse racing it includes the attendant gambling, the whole culture of breeding, training and riding horses, weighing their jockeys, and so on.

Even visually there are cultural factors that lead to a horse race being selectively presented by the caller. In a horse race there is one sequence of physical events, the race with its start and finish and the events between. Clearly the caller perceives this race, but only some of the events of the race are culturally significant. These can be seen as occurring in perceptual overlays. The actual events take place in the physical world in three dimensions (four if time is included). Jockeys sit on top of horses. They can fall off and sometimes do. Horses bound along in a gallop going up and down. But it is not culturally significant that the horses and riders are going up and down, except in those circumstances when a horse and/or rider falls. Insofar as it matters culturally, there are two overlay races taking place when horses race at a racetrack. In one, horses are viewed as if from the air. This is a two-dimensional race. The whole field is moving around the track and individual horses are moving faster or slower than average and changing their positions relative to each other. Some horses are closer to the rail and others are further out on the track. Not everything about this overlay is of cultural significance. For example some tracks are run clockwise and some counterclockwise, some are more or less oval, some more circular. During the race, commentators do not mention these facts because they do not matter to the race as race. But they do mention whether horses are *inside* or *outside* one another in the two-dimensional race.

The second culturally significant overlay is one-dimensional. Here horses run in sequence from the start to the finish, and are first, second, third, and so forth. This one-dimensional race is the one on which there is gambling and about which commentary is most significant. The importance of the one-dimensional overlay can be seen from the fact that being the first horse past the finishing post on the far side of the track is of no significance whatsoever if eight other horses passed the finishing post earlier on the inside of the track although it may be that the outside horse has run a longer race and is therefore in actual meters or yards covered in the time, the fastest runner.

The discourse rules and formulae closely reflect the two culturally determined overlays of the physical events. As noted, the only time a commentator mentions the vertical dimension is when a rider has a fall. A fall influences the possible outcome of the one-dimensional race because one rider at least will not be a contender. The rest of the time the discourse structure codes only the one-dimensional overlay of the race.

Consider again the discourse structure of race calling in play-by-play commentary mode in Fig. 2.1. The rules provide for the order of the horses to be repeatedly given, with the prefinish cycles showing that the significant part of the race is the end, and the significant horses are the first group of runners. This priority is a cultural one and is also underlined by the fact that gambling is associated with the one-dimensional race. If horse racing were a kind of equine ballet, then the commentary would not stress the first three place getters but the grace of a particular horse and possibly its ability to perform certain interesting movements.

The formulae of race calling code aspects of both the one-dimensional and the two-dimensional overlays. Look, for example, at the two formulae typically used by Reon Murtha to indicate that he is looping back to start at the head of the field again. He might say, *Round the turn they come* or *400 meters left to go.* The first formula, *Round the turn they come,* is an indication of where the horses are in the two-dimensional race, that is, where on the oval track. The second, *400 left to run,* is an indication of where they are in the one-dimensional race because no mention is made of the fact that the 400 meters are not in a straight line. There are even individual words that can be assigned to one race or the other. The word *home,* which occurs in a number of formulae, such as *They head for home* and *600 meters from home,* locates a place in the one-dimensional overlay, namely the finishing post. The word *there* often locates the other end of the one-dimensional overlay, namely the start, in formulae such as *Just about there.* On the other hand, the verb *parked* is always used to locate a horse in two dimensions in formulae such as *parked on the outside, parked three wide, parked next to X.* The only word that seems to belong exclusively to the horizontal dimension is an intransitive *down* in formulae like *X is down.* (A horse that is *down* has fallen.)

The denizens of the racetrack take these ways of seeing races for granted. It follows that commentators exclude and to some extent occlude. They can say only certain things and in only certain ways. They are limited by the way their culture expects them to represent and re-present events.

Commentators of slower sports like cricket seem not to be as limited in the way they speak as race callers even though both relate what they see in culturally appropriate ways. Cricket commentators can mention the size of the crowd, whether a player is doing warming up exercises or has gotten his gear dirty by sliding in the field, matters having little to do with the competitive nature of the game or its major episodes. They do not normally remark on whether a player is chewing gum or scratching his or her nose, matters that seem similarly irrelevant. This suggests that play-by-play commentary in race calling is restricted by additional factors. These factors, I suggest, cause speakers to restrict themselves to the linguistic features of formulaic speech.

Processing and Memory Pressures During Play-By-Play Commentary

To understand why it is that the linguistic choices available to a commentator must be reduced during play-by-play commentary, we look at just what it is the commentator is expected to do. Consider what a race caller has to remember during the calling of a race. The race is being run while the commentator is in play-by-play mode. This makes demands on the caller's memory. At a minimum, he must store the following things in long-term memory (LTM):[5]

1. A list of the names of all the horses that are running.
2. Linked with this list, the colors of each horse, that is, the colors of the owner or trainer that the jockey or driver wears.
3. Linked with List 1, the name of each jockey/driver of each horse.
4. Linked with List 1, the name(s) of the owner(s).
5. Linked with List 1, the name(s) of the trainer(s).
6. Linked with List 1, a list of the favorite(s) for the race.
7. The length of the race.
8. The physical nature of the track and the names of its topographical features.
9. The current state of the track.

These items are stored in memory. The evidence for this is that they may be required at any time during the race in order to make the commentary possible and

---

[5]The distinction between long-term memory and short-term or working memory is a longstanding one in research on memory. I suppose with Miller (1956) that working memory is quite small, whereas long-term memory is unfillable in a finite lifetime, and access from it is very rapid. See Newell and Simon (1972) for an early but explicit account of how such a division of labor in memory might be modeled.

written notes could not be referred to fast enough to maintain the abnormal fluency that commentators do. Furthermore, all of the items appear in commentaries of races. For example, if the caller did not know the length of the race he would not know how much further the race had to run. Yet this is required in order to fill the loop formulae with the appropriate content, for example, the formula *x left to run* where x is the distance from the finish.

Race calling involves minimally the following actions and associated working memory and processing operations:

1. Watching the race through field glasses.

2. On the basis of the colors and physical features of each horse, recalling the name of the horse and when required the name of its jockey, trainer, and owner from LTM.

3. Discerning for each horse its relative and measured position both in a linear sequence, if horses are one behind the other, and in two dimensions, if horses are traveling one outside the other. The relative position is the position of the horse relative to some other in purely positional terms, that is, one horse is in front of, beside, behind, another. Measured position is given in specialist dimensions such as lengths, necks, or noses.

4. Discerning the current location of each horse. (Note that location is both position on the track as a physical [elliptical] entity and position in the race as a linear entity with a start at its beginning and finish at its end.)

5. Discerning changes in relative and absolute position.

6. Noting any unusual happenings such as horses or riders falling, infringements of good racing behavior, and the like.

Let us suppose that commentators have, at any one time, a perceptual window in which the salient items are a horse under current scrutiny; the horses immediately in front, beside, and behind it; and the location of each horse relative to the others in two dimensions. In the perceptual window too is the field's location on the track (e.g., in the back straight, which is the straight at the far side of the track away from the main stands, or on the showgrounds bend); and in the race dimensions (e.g., at the 1,500-meter mark). What is in the perceptual window changes in two ways. The commentator changes what is in the window by moving the window through the field from the first horse to the last and then back to the first horse again, that is, the window is moved cyclically through the field of runners. But the view through the window changes while the commentator is speaking. The relative location of the whole field itself changes in two ways. First, it moves around the track and, second, from the start to the finish of the race. That is always the case. At any time the participants in the window may change their relative positions.

At the same time, events outside the current window may occasionally be significant enough to override the attention being placed there; the commentator may sometimes switch at a split second's notice to describing some event outside the current window, but this is not always the case. For example, Reon Murtha in conversation with me described a situation in which he was concentrating on the last few hundred yards of the race, calling only the first few horses. At this point two horses fell at the back of the field, an occurrence that he did not observe but one that was seen by most other people on the course. The use of binoculars by the caller at times does occlude peripheral events. This is a necessary requirement for attending to his task, and in this case events outside his field of vision did not override Murtha's commentary.

Although in all such performance situations working memory is heavily engaged in nonlinguistic activities, the commentator is required to speak fluently all the while. As Fodor, Bever, and Garrett (1974) showed, speaking also requires working memory space. So what is it about oral formulaic performance that makes it a suitable response to such a situation? Formulaic speech cuts down the number of choices available to the speaker and consequently reduces the amount of linguistic information that must be retained in working memory and linguistic processing that must be done while still allowing for the speaker to maintain a high level of fluency.

How does formulaic speech produce this result? The commentator must process incoming visual stimuli and produce outgoing commentary almost instantaneously. The commentary must also be fluent. Because the game is seen as a limited number of set moves, the play-by-play commentary can be coded in a fixed discourse structure and an inventory of formulae, each of which is indexed for constituents of the discourse. Let us suppose that formulae are contained in a file box and that each one is filed under a heading and that the heading is, in turn, a label in a discourse structure rule. The commentator then needs only to select one formula after another, in the order dictated by the label on each formula matched to the circumstance he is relating, to get a perfect account of the events. This is an idealized picture of what happens, of course, but it seems to be a possible and plausible explanation of the facts of oral formulaic performance.

According to this theory, as pressure of time on sports commentators increases they should increasingly revert to using formulae. This is supported by a study conducted by Wanta and Meggett (1988), whose survey of the use of clichés by college football commentators in the United States shows that "announcers tended to use more clichés when the game deviated from the expected outcome. Announcers also tended to use more clichés in games involving teams that were highly ranked" (p. 87). The probability of an upset result for a high-ranking team puts greater pressure on the commentator because at such times the tension toward the conclusion of the game is raised and the impending result requires more processing to explain it.

What then of droned or chanted intonation, which I have mentioned as a feature of the commentary of rapid sports? It too cuts down the number of choices the speaker must make. In normal speech, a speaker must plan ahead, and ahead of or at the same time as this planning, must also plan an intonation tune for what is being said. A drone makes this localized planning unnecessary. As we have also seen, the race caller drones or chants in a predetermined way. The curve of pitch rises is fixed and instead of needing to be adjusted for each sentence or subpart of a sentence, is set for the whole of the play-by-play section of the commentary.

If the preceding explanation is correct, then the abnormal fluency achieved by the race commentator, although required of him, is also a direct consequence of the performance technique he uses. If we suppose that the performance of a play-by-play commentator is in some sense automated, involving the selection of formulae in a partly predetermined order, then we would not expect the speaker to speed up and slow down at clause boundaries because at such boundaries the speaker is not planning a new clause but has already selected the next formula. Commentators of fast sports in fact do not pause and have an even articulation rate. For the same reason, the speaker does not need to hesitate or use filler words and phrases. Therefore, he can be abnormally fluent. The more proficient he becomes, the more fluent he will also become because the processes of accessing formulae from long-term memory will become increasingly rapid.

How much predictive power has this theory? To find that out we need to look further afield to see if memory loading and processing pressures always interact with the appearance of formulaic speech in the way the theory predicts. This analysis is performed in chapter 3 through consideration of the discourse of various auctioneers.

3

The Speech of Auctioneers

We are now in a position to test the hypothesis of the previous chapter, namely that when speakers are under heavy pressure from having to perform activities other than speaking they do so using formulaic resources. To test this hypothesis I compare the speech of sports callers with that of auctioneers. Auctioneering and sports calling are quite different "speech registers" (Biber & Finegan, 1993), as we shall see, and those who perform in one register do not normally perform in the other. So if there are striking similarities between these two kinds of speech, then we cannot attribute those to a common origin or parallel participation and must seek explanations elsewhere.

Why select the speech of auctioneers for this comparison? The speech of auctioneers is particularly appropriate because auctions contain many relevant variables. All auctions are routines and all auctioneers are under some degree of pressure from sources other than those to do with their having to speak. Such pressures include having to scan the bench of buyers for bids, and to recall the details of the lot and the current highest bid. But the degree of pressure varies from one auction tradition to another—from real estate to wool, from tobacco to fine art. For example, I was told by Kent Prior, a Christchurch real estate auctioneer, that at some real estate auctions in Australia the auctioneer may take bidders aside and tell them that they are not trying hard enough to effect a purchase. In this regard, real estate auctioneers do not have to speak rapidly. They usually sell only one lot per sale, so the rate of sale is slow and the rate at which the auctioneer is required to speak is also relatively normal.

At the other end of the pressure scale are the tobacco auctions of the southern United States, where auctioneers sell thousands of lots in a day at a rate of about one lot every 5 seconds. Tobacco auctioneers are required to speak rapidly because of intense time pressure constraints.

In the middle of the pressure scale are the antique auctions conducted by general auctioneers and livestock sales. Lots are sold there once every 30 to 90 seconds, a good many lots are sold at one time, and speakers are expected to be fluent.

If the various features of formulaic speech are present in the same circumstances in auctions as in the speech of sports commentators, then the theory proposed in the previous chapter predicts that formulaic speech features will be most densely clustered at the high-pressure end of the scale and less in evidence at the low-pressure end. I use the rate of sale as a proxy measure for the pressure the auctioneer faces. I suppose that the rate of sale results from traditional factors that place the auctioneer under pressure to sell at a particular pace. A slow rate of sale equates to relatively little pressure on the auctioneer to sell, whereas a fast-paced auction places the auctioneer under considerable pressure. I support this use of rate of sale as a proxy as we explore a range of auction situations.

THE RITUAL CONTEXT

Auctions are rituals. People come together at an appointed time and an appointed place. They perform a series of acts that are, for the most part, predetermined. In this respect, auctions are like church services. The practical function of an auction ritual is that goods are bought and sold, but there are also a number of other functions for this ritual. For example, it sets prices, it allocates goods to particular buyers in preference to others, and it allows those who wish to become known for their ownership of particular items to achieve their ownership publicly (Smith, 1989).

Auctions are not just economic events, but also socially and culturally significant events. They often bring together people who know each other in a context in which they transact business communally. To understand something of this context for auctioning we can look at the events surrounding the Whately Cooperative Livestock Auction in Whately, Massachusetts. This auction, which I attended in 1981, is a particularly good example because it is a very colorful event.

The building in which the auction was conducted is a rather ramshackle one with livestock pens outside. Inside there is a small amphitheater with tiered wooden seating on one side of a sawdust-filled arena. On the other side of the arena is the auctioneer's box. The auctioneer on the November 24, 1981 was Milt Crosby, a general auctioneer from New York State who at that time came up about once a month to conduct the Whately auction; he carried an ornate stick in his hand and wore boots and a stetson. The buyers were dressed for the cold; they had on padded jackets and woollen hats of various designs and colors. They were of various ethnic origins: Poles and Portuguese, often whole families for whom this was an outing. Many of the buyers were also vendors, and it was clear that they frequently met at the auction. They talked from the time the sale opened in the morning to the time it closed in the evening.

When Milt Crosby first climbed into the box and turned on the microphone he sold small livestock: rabbits, chickens, eggs, and ducks, each brought in through the door to his right. The public address system crackled, its electronic fidelity leaving a lot to be desired. The lot was held up for all to see and when the hammer fell it was taken out through the door to the auctioneer's left. People drifted in and out of the amphitheater. They smoked, dozed, read the paper, went to eat in the attached cafe, and some of them bid. Usually they bid for each other's produce.

Only late in the day, when the cattle were auctioned, was there a significant presence of professional buyers. As the lots got bigger, the auction became more animated. One huge goat excited a great deal of comment as it was bought by a Portuguese butcher for his customers. All the while Milt Crosby provided amusing descriptions of the beasts on sale. He directed comments to regulars and cajoled bids from reluctant buyers.

As at all auctions I have studied, the people at the Whately auction celebrate the operation of the free market in which they all participate. They appraise each other's stock. They make decisions about whether or not to buy. The vendors have already made the decision to sell, having earlier made their own appraisal of the beasts they wish to sell and the state of the market. The auction allows them to test whether their appraisal was right or not. It allows them to compare their product with that of their competitors and then to give it a monetary value. Occasionally, they may complain that an injustice has been done, but, for the most part, they show by their presence and the fact that they buy and sell at auction that they have faith in their market. They believe in it and once a month they celebrate that belief collectively.

Smith (1989) showed how central such belief is:

> To many people, including most economists, the idea that auctions function to establish a "fair" price is incontrovertible; by their definition, the auction price is both correct and fair since it is the price at which market supply and demand curves cross. This particular view of fair value, however, only has meaning within the economic paradigm. "Fairness" for most people connotes something more; it implies a governing principle of legitimacy grounded within the community. It is not merely the product of rational individual decision makers, it is a social goal. (p. 80)[1]

It is clear by the definition of a ritual in chapter 1 that such an event is a ritual.

The speech of the auctioneer guides and directs the whole of this ritual. The men in the yards bring beasts in as the auctioneer requires. They take them out when he has finished. The clerical staff in the office upstairs makes out the bills as the auction proceeds.

Mundane auctions like this one are performed in many parts of the English-speaking world and for a great variety of commodities. Koenig (1972–1973) provided a detailed description of the ritual elements of cattle auctions in Texas. Smith (1989) gave accounts of fish auctions in Boston, book rights auctions in New York City, and race horse auctions in Kentucky. Cassady (1967) traveled the world attending a great variety of fish auctions. Harris (1993) gave a detailed ethnography of a variety of auctions in Melbourne, Australia.

At the other end of the social spectrum from the Whately Cooperative Livestock Auction are the great auction houses of Sotheby's and Christie's, dealing in lots worth millions of dollars. Sotheby's advertises for lots and its reputation alone is enough to attract potential vendors of van Goghs and Stradivarii. It also has the

---

[1]Although there are no crises of confidence there is evidence that some auction markets are economically inefficient (Peterson & Georgianna, 1988; Smith, 1989).

technical staff to perform appraisals of such rare and valuable items. Its catalogs provide information that is needed for buyers to make an appraisal of their own. The fact that an item is to be sold by Sotheby's and has the firm's authentication allows the market to be as sure as it can be that the product is rather less subject to the vagaries of *caveat emptor* than would be the case elsewhere.

The auctioneer plays a quasi-priestly function in the auction ceremony. He conducts the ritual and pronounces the required words. At the high point of the ceremony, he pronounces the words and performs the actions that are binding on the participants. His words and actions have the sanction of law as well as of custom. The auctioneer is bound by the laws of agency and contract, as are the buyer and vendor.[2] When the auctioneer bangs his gavel, a legally binding contract is made.

Auctioneers are also themselves operating in their own free market of auctioneers. Those who sell well attract higher wages. They attract the better lots and so, at the same time as they serve as agents for their vendors, they are selling themselves.

NONLINGUISTIC PRESSURES ON AUCTIONEERS

All auctioneers are engaged in a range of nonlinguistic tasks at the same time as they are speaking. Some central tasks are common to all auctioneers. The main one is that of bid spotting. Any gallery or bench of buyers contains potential bidders. Because, in many traditions, bidding is difficult to discern (to keep the identity of the highest bidder secret from others), the auctioneer must concentrate hard to see who is bidding. At the same time, all auctioneers must remember where they are in the bidding sequence. Sometimes this is relatively simple, as in the case of tobacco auctions where only three digits (representing a number of dollars and cents) need to be remembered. But in other auctioning traditions pressures on the auctioneer's memory and processing are complex arising out of a variety of factors. Like commentators, auctioneers are also under pressure to react instantly. The moment they see a bid they must react to drive the market on and signal accurately to all the potential buyers what is currently the highest bid.

One manifestation of these pressures is the attentiveness of auctioneers. They concentrate hard on what they are doing, particularly in the scanning of buyers for signs of bids. The larger the bench of buyers the more difficult that is. If there is a large gallery, as in some antique auctions, the auctioneer may be assisted by people whose sole task it is to spot bids. To avoid confusion between the auctioneer and the spotters, various bidders are assigned informally to each spotter. On one hand, having others spot the potential buyers splits up the task. On the other hand, it creates a problem for the auctioneer in keeping track of who is covering which bidder.

Auctioneers are also affected by characteristics of the buyers. An entirely professional bench of buyers demands that the auctioneer be expeditious and

---

[2]Powell (1961) and Treitel (1970) cover the auctioneer's legal obligations under the laws of agency and contract.

professional. In contrast, an amateur gallery of buyers expects the auctioneer to lead, instruct, and sometimes to entertain, which means the same degree of expedition is not possible.

The pacing of an auction also creates pressure on an auctioneer. An auction must keep moving at a steady pace. This pace varies, but no auction can afford to stall for more than a few seconds. It is up to the auctioneer to keep up the rhythm of bidding by the rhythm with which he calls the bids. The optimal auction, from the auctioneer's perspective, is where there is a bid for every bid called, a bid call for every bid, and no delay in obtaining the next bid. If five people bid at once, that creates as much difficulty as no one bidding. In the first case, the auctioneer must make order out of the bidding where there is no order. In the second, he must fill the space left by the absence of bidding either by repeating the call of the previously highest bid, or else by some interpolation that avoids the appearance of there being a gap. So, like the race caller, the auctioneer cannot break down. He has a rhythm that he must maintain even though that rhythm is often not matched by the rhythm of bidding.

Auctioneers also have legal responsibilities that create pressure on them for complete accuracy in a number of matters. These include knowing which is currently the highest bid, who has bid it, and what the reserve price is. If an auctioneer makes mistakes in any of these areas he will, at best, look inept and he may even be subject to legal action by parties to the sale.

These pressures are shared by all auctioneers, but there are additional ones for some auctioneers; on the basis of these additional demands, auctions can be roughly ranked on a pressure continuum as noted earlier. I begin by looking at the ends of the pressure continuum to see what features of formulaic speech are in evidence there, and then move to the middle of the continuum. Recall that we are using the auctioneer's rate of sale as a proxy measure for the amount of pressure an auctioneer is under.

LOW RATE OF SALE AUCTIONS

A Real Estate Auction

I begin with the example of an auction conducted in the Real Estate Rooms of Wrightson NMA, Christchurch, New Zealand, recorded on March 11, 1982. For about a month the house being offered at auction had been advertised in the local newspaper. People interested in buying it traveled to the village of Leeston outside Christchurch to inspect it with the real estate agent. Now those who are interested in bidding on it are gathered in the real estate company's offices for the property to be put up for sale. The land sales room is poorly lit, with little natural light, and is noisy because it has no carpets and drapes. It is sparsely furnished with just a couple of rows of seats in which about 20 people are seated on this particular day.

The auctioneer begins by reading aloud and at speed the terms and conditions of sale under which the auction is to be conducted. These terms and conditions are the legal framework indicating exactly what everyone is or is not permitted to do and the legal consequences of their actions.

Then the auction commences. The auctioneer, Rod Cameron, briefly describes the property, noting what he regards as its major attractions and then calls for a first bid at the figure of $90,000. After obtaining a first bid at a lower level he calls the bids, initially in set denominations as they are made by the buyers, later in smaller increments, indicating from time to time the location of the bidder. Toward the end of the bid calling the bidding slows and he pauses several times for periods of some seconds. Then the point is reached where the vendor is asked if the property has reached a high enough price to be sold. She indicates that it has and the sale is made by the drop of the gavel. The sale price is only $2,000 higher than the figure initially nominated by the auctioneer for a trial first bid. The auctioneer then congratulates the buyer and thanks the bidders for their contribution to the auction. The section of the auction in the transcript, excluding the reading of the conditions of sale, lasted 223 seconds. It was the only auction conducted. The rate of sale is thus 1 sale in 223 seconds. The following is a transcript of the auction.[3]

I.1   Well ladies and gentlemen,
        {2-second pause}
        we're offering today
        I'm sorry, are there any questions on the conditions of
I.5   sale?
        {6-second pause}
        We're offering today, ladies and gentlemen,
        this very fine house in Leeston which
        {4-second pause}
I.10   Mr. O'Boyle ah built some 16 odd years ago and
        recognizably one of the best homes built in Leeston ah
        It has many
        {3-second pause}
        outstanding features as those who have inspected it of
I.15   course will realize.
        It's on a very large section of twelve hundred and
        forty-one square meters which um on the old
        {2-second pause}
        measures is forty-eight perches.
I.20   {clears throat}
        The garden, of course, is ah mature and well-
        established.
        I will not dwell on describing the house.

[3]The reading of the terms and conditions of sale has been left out of the transcript because it is not relevant to the formulaic performance of an auctioneer.

Most of those present will have inspected the same, and
I.25   they will know the quality of the fittings and the
furnishings that go with it.
Without any further ado, I will put the property up for
auction.
Has anybody got me ninety thousand dollars to start?
I.30   {4-second pause}
Eighty-five?
{4-second pause}
Seventy-five thousand?
{5-second pause}
I.35   Right, sixty-five thousand dollars to start me.
I have sixty-five thousand dollars.
I will take five thousand dollar rises.
I have sixty-five thousand dollar bid.
I have sixty-five thousand dollars.
I.40   Sixty-five thousand dollars.
Seventy thousand.
Thank you.
I have seventy thousand dollars.
I have seventy thousand dollars.
I.45   I have seventy thousand dollar bid.
At seventy thousand dollars.
{Assistant: Yes.}
Seventy-five thousand.
At seventy-five thousand.
I.50   Seventy-five thousand bid.
At seventy-five.
At seventy sssss seven
at the back there.
Thank you.
I.55   At seventy-seven thousand.
At seventy-seven thousand.
Round up, Sir?
{Assistant: Eighty.}
Eighty.
I.60   I have eighty thousand dollars.
The bid is direct in front of me.
I have eighty thousand dollars.
Eighty-two thousand.
I have eighty-two thousand.
I.65   I have eighty-two thousand.
{Assistant: Four.}
Four thousand.

I have eighty-four thousand.
Eighty-six thousand.
I.70   Eighty-six thousand dollars.
At eighty-six thousand dollars.
{2-second pause}
It's a beautiful property.
You can't mistake it.
I.75   {1-second pause}
It's a very well
Eighty-six thousand dollars.
{3-second pause &
Assistant: Yes.}
I.80   Eighty-eight.
At eighty-eight thousand dollars.
At eighty-eight.
At eighty-eight.
{4-second pause}
I.85   Come on now.
At eighty-eight thousand.
I'll take a thousand dollars.
{2-second pause}
Thank you.
I.90   Eighty-nine.
At eighty-nine thousand dollars.
{Assistant: Yes.}
At ninety thousand dollars.
I have ninety thousand dollars, Jim,
I.95   Direct to me.
At ninety thousand dollars.
{2-second pause}
You coming again, Sir?
Ninety-one thousand.
I.100   At ninety-one thousand.
{Assistant: Yes.}
At ninety-two thousand.
At ninety-two thousand dollars.
At ninety-two thousand dollars.
I.105   Ninety-two thousand dollars.
You can't build it.
It would cost well in excess of that.
Ninety-two thousand dollars.
{8-second pause}
I.110   Is the property on the market, Mrs. eh Miss Neil?
{5-second pause}

{Assistant: The property is on the market.}
The property is on the market?
{Vendor's reply: Yes.}
I.115   Thank you.
I have ninety-two thousand direct in front of me.
I have ninety-two thousand for the first time.
{4-second pause}
I have ninety-two thousand for the second time.
I.120   {3-second pause}
I have ninety-two thousand for the third and final time.
Your last chance.
{5-second pause}
{Gavel drop}
I.125   Thank you, Sir.
Extremely well purchased.
Thank you, ladies and gentlemen, for your attendance and
your spirited bidding.

From the text and its description a clear structure can be induced. The auction
starts with a description of the lot (Lines I.1–26). Then follows the search for a first
bid (Lines I.27–34). In this case the auctioneer puts up a number of possible first
bids in descending order. When he has obtained a first bid there follows a period
during which he calls bids (Lines I.35–109). The bid calling contains interpolations
(e.g., Lines I.57–58, I.73–74). Some of these are from his assistant who is spotting
bids for the auctioneer. Some are addresses to parties to the auction, to bidders, and
at one stage to the vendor. They also include further descriptions of the lot. There
are pauses from time to time. Toward the end of the bid calling the auctioneer checks
with the vendor to see that the property is "on the market," that is, has reached a
sufficiently high price for the vendor to be prepared to sell it at that price or a higher
one (Lines I.110–115). Further bidding follows and the bid calling concludes with
a version of the formula *going once, going twice, third and last time,* after which
the gavel falls and the sale is made. In a short epilogue the auctioneer congratulates
the buyer and thanks the other bidders (Lines I.125–129).

Auctions are not like commentaries in that there are no external events to narrate.
Instead, the auctioneer creates the verbal framework within which external events,
such as the holding aloft of a lot at an antique auction, take place. Thus, the structure
of an auction is its discourse structure. The rules for it are given in Fig. 3.1.

Much of Rod Cameron's auction consists of formulae. Here again is a
minidictionary of some of them.

1. Description of the lot:
    a. we/I are/am offering today   (I.3)
    b. ladies and gentlemen   (I.1, I.7, I.127)
    c. fittings and furnishings   (I.25–26)

R 1 Auction ----> Description of the lot + opening bid search + bid calling + sale +

    (epilogue)

R 2 Bid calling ---> bid 1 + bid 2 + ... + bid n

FIG. 3.1. Discourse structure rules for auctions.

2. Opening bid search:
   a. I will put the property up for sale/auction. (I.27–28)
   b. Has anyone got me X dollars to start me? (I.29)
3. Bid calling:
   a. At X dollars.
   b. I have X dollars.
4. Bid locator:
   a. The bid's in front/on the aisle/at the back/direct to me. (I.53, I.61)
5. Interpolations:
   a. Come on now. (I.85)
   b. You coming again, Sir? (I.98)

A High-Class Antique Auction

In the elegant sale rooms of Sotheby's in Belgravia (London, England), auctions proceed in a similar fashion as far as the discourse structure is concerned but without the "extras" to which Rod Cameron had to resort to advance the bidding. In Belgravia one does not cajole the buyers; the buyers are, after all, either very rich or professional buyers of antiques, and Sotheby's is one of the most respected auction houses in the world. The recording on which the following transcript is based was made at Sotheby's in Belgravia on January 6, 1982 by Douglas C. Haggo. The auctioneer is not known. The auction lasted for 76 seconds and one rug was sold in that time. The rate of sale is thus 1 sale in 76 seconds.

II.1   Lot 66 the senna rug on my left
    {3-second pause}
    woven on silk.
    {2-second pause}
II.5   Twelve hundred pound starting this.
    Twelve hundred.
    {4-second pause}
    Thirteen hundred.
    {2-second pause}
II.10   Fourteen hundred.
    {2-second pause}
    Fifteen hundred.
    {2-second pause}

	Sixteen hundred.
II.15	{3-second pause}
	Seventeen hundred.
	Eighteen hundred.
	Nineteen hundred.
	{1-second pause}
II.20	Nineteen hundred.
	Two thousand.
	Two thousand pound.
	{1-second pause}
	At two thousand pound.
II.25	Two thousand two hundred.
	{2-second pause}
	Two thousand three and four hundred.
	{3-second pause}
	Two thousand five hundred.
II.30	{2-second pause}
	Two thousand six hundred.
	{3-second pause}
	Two thousand seven hundred.
	{3-second pause}
II.35	Two thousand eight hundred.
	{6-second pause}
	Two thousand eight hundred pound.
	{2-second pause}
	At two thousand eight hundred pound.
II.40	Any more?
	Two thousand eight hundred pound.
	{1-second pause}
	Against you.
	Two thousand.
II.45	{Assistant: Nine hundred.}
	Two thousand nine hundred.
	{1-second pause}
	At two thousand nine hundred.
	The bid is now on the aisle.
II.50	At two thousand nine hundred.
	{1-second pause}
	Two thousand nine hundred.
	Your bid.
	{gavel fall}
II.55	Two thousand nine hundred.
	Harold.

Properties and Discourse Structure of Low-Pressure Auctions

Both real estate auctions and the auctioning of high-class antiques are at the low-pressure end of the scale in terms of the processing pressure they place on auctioneers. On average, both have a rate of sale of slower than one sale per minute.

The discourse organization of the antique auction is identical to the real estate auction in its macro structure. I presuppose that the discourse of auctioning, like that of sports commentaries, has hierarchical organization. Recall that I discussed the nature of this kind of organization of temporal events in chapter 1. The antique auction, like the real estate auction, begins with a description of the lot, albeit a much shorter one (Lines II.1–4). There is then an opening bid search (Line II.5) after which the bids are called (Lines II.6–53). When the auctioneer feels he has no more bids coming, a sale is made by the dropping of the gavel after which he names the sale price and the buyer (Lines II.55–56).

Some of the micro structure is also similar across both auctions. Both auctioneers occasionally locate the bid in space. In the real estate auction, the auctioneer indicates that a particular bid is direct to him or comes from "at the back there" (Line I.53). The Sotheby's auctioneer says that "the bid is now on the aisle" (Line II.49). By doing so both auctioneers also indicate from time to time where the current highest bidder is located. At other times they indicate the current highest bidder more directly, as in "direct to me" or "your bid" (Lines I.95, II.53). Notice that these bid locator formulae are interpolated at points where the bidding is not proceeding at normal pace, particularly near the end of the bid calling when the auctioneer wishes there to be no doubt about which is the current highest bid and bidder. Both auctioneers also indicate toward the end of the auction that the auction is drawing to a close. One asks, "Any more?" (Line II.40). The other says, "Your last chance" (Line I.122).

The way these interpolations are made is through formulae. One can hear *Any more?* or *Any more bids?* in many auctions, but this is not all. The whole of the bid calling phase of the auction is made up of formulae. Look at the way the bids themselves are called. Rod Cameron, who sold the house in the real estate auction described earlier, used the following formulae to call bids:

1. I have X dollar bid
   I have X dollars
   X dollars
   X
   (where X is a dollar value.)
2. At X dollars
   At X

These are rather simple and repetitive ways to call bids. They are clearly formulae to judge from their repeated use and from the fact that there are no other

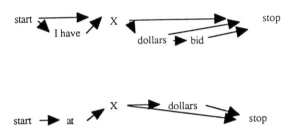

FIG. 3.2. Finite state diagrams of two bid calling formulae.

expressions used for calling the bids. The Sotheby's auctioneer's inventory of bidding formulae is even simpler. He uses only the second set of formulae given (converted into English currency) as in the following:

3. At X pounds
    X pounds
    X

How should we explain the arbitrary form of these formulae and their variants? Let us look again at Cameron's simple means of bid calling and let us suppose that the different forms of formulae sets 1 and 2 are not themselves formulae but variant forms of the same formula. In each case, some of the elements are compulsory and some optional. We can account for this by supposing that many formulae are generated by finite state grammars without loops (i.e., without the possibility of returning to or repeating earlier elements). A finite state grammar can be thought of as a kind of machine that moves from state to state, emitting a word along the way at each state. Such machines are finite because they permit only a very limited number of grammatically acceptable utterances to be produced. Finite state grammars can be given in the form of diagrams that look like those in Fig. 3.2.[4]

I suppose from now on that all formulae are finite state systems of this type. This allows for an important distinction to be made. The formula as a finite state diagram is part of a speaker's competence, that is, part of the set of linguistic resources that he or she has at his or her command. When such a formula is accessed from memory and used in an appropriate situational context, it becomes part of performance (see chap. 1). To mirror this distinction I have used the typographical convention, mentioned in an earlier footnote, of placing all performed formulae in quotation marks where I know them to have been spoken as an utterance. Otherwise, they are in italics and are to be treated as idealized utterances within the grammar.

---

[4]The likelihood that formulae are finite state explains why some variants appear and not others. It is because only those linguistic forms generable by the finite state diagrams are available variants. Formulae share this property with idioms (Chafe, 1968; Di Sciullo & Williams, 1987; Fraser, 1970; Weinreich, 1969).

Returning now to finite state diagrams, a simple way to look at such a diagram is to suppose that a speaker starts at the left-hand end and then follows any single track of arrows through the diagram, uttering the words that he or she passes on the way to the stop sign at the right-hand end. A finite state representation allows for the explicit presentation of the fact that many things that auctioneers say are variant forms of each other.

Both auctioneers whose words are contained in the previous transcripts are fluent. During the bid calling there are no hesitations: no voiced or unvoiced hesitation pauses, no anacolutha (false starts), and no filler words and phrases. There is one point at which Cameron is not sure what the bid is and holds the initial consonant of the word *seven* until he is sure he has the next bid (Line I.52). This is not a hesitation so much as a delay in speaking. However, during the description of the lot Cameron has a number of hesitation pauses, some voiced and some unvoiced (Lines I.9, 10, 11, 13, 17, 18, 21).

During the bid calling both auctioneers have what might be called delay pauses rather than hesitation pauses. For example in Lines I.30, 32, 34, 72, 75, 78, 84, 88, 97, 109, 111, 118, 120, 123 and II.2, 4, 7, 9, 11, 13, 15, 19, 23, 26, 28, 30, 32, 34, 36, 38, 42, 47, 52, the auctioneer is not hesitating by delaying the onset of what he says next. Given how regularly these pauses are paced in the speech of the Sotheby's auctioneer, they appear to be used as a kind of rhythmic device for setting the pace of the bidding. In Cameron's case, during some of the pauses he is waiting for an opening bid near the beginning of the auction. Near the end of the auction, he is waiting for the next bid.

In brief, both the auctioneers in these slow-paced auctions are fluent and this fluency, I propose, is related to their use of formulae.

Neither auctioneer drones. Both of them use normal speech intonation and stress, but in a restricted way. The Sotheby's auctioneer, for example, uses the same intonation tune bid after bid. On each of a sequence of bids where only a single integer rises in value, the intonation has a falling tune on the new integer. This tune is graphically represented by the two examples in Fig. 3.3. To interpret this notation imagine that the top and bottom lines are the normal top and bottom of a speaker's intonational range and that the black dots are notes. The tail represents the pitch change direction of the nuclear syllable (Crystal, 1969).

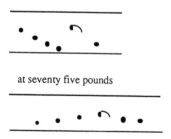

at seventy five pounds

two thousand eight hundred

FIG. 3.3. Intonation melodies used by a Sotheby's auctioneer.

FIG. 3.4. Presale intonation melody
used by a Sotheby's auctioneer.

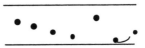

Toward the end of the bidding there will be at least one bid call with a rising tune. This rising tune indicates that the gavel may fall from then on. This tune is represented in Fig. 3.4.

Cameron's intonation is similarly restricted to a smaller than normal range of intonational possibilities, but he also does not drone or chant.

The rate at which these two auctioneers speak is also normal. It seems they are not required to be extraordinarily fluent in the way that race callers are, and so no requirement to drone is imposed on them.

Conclusion

The auctioneers in these two kinds of auction appear to be under relatively low pressure. The rate at which they sell in lots per second is not particularly fast; they apparently have a reasonable time to sell what there is to sell. The rhythm of the bid calling is not rapid. They take bids as they come. Neither of them is left for long periods without bids, the Sotheby's sale being particularly easy on the auctioneer in this respect. A slow bidding rate means that the auctioneer has time to register a bid in memory and to take note of any other bidders who may still be bidding. Because the auctioneer does not need to speak rapidly, with bids coming regularly, and because he is not under pressure to sell rapidly, he has time to perform speech processing tasks.

It seems that the auctioneers of low-pressure (low sale rate) auctions use the discourse structure common to all auctions. They use a small number of formulae sporadically, but they do not seem to have many in their repertoire. This is predicted by the hypothesis that the evolution of formulae is in part a response to psychological pressure on speech processing. Because such auctioneers are not under much pressure, they do not need to evolve a large store of formulae for all eventualities. Normal speech will do if auctioneers in a low-pressure tradition become stuck. They are fluent but without many of the features of abnormal fluency that race callers have. They do not have the race caller's even articulation rate and they do have hesitation pauses. They do not drone, although their intonation patterns are relatively limited. In their description of the lot, they speak with the features of normally fluent speech.

These characteristics of low-pressure auction speech are predicted by the theory that says that features of formulaic speech are a response to processing and working memory pressure in routine contexts. These auctioneers are not under great pressure and some of the linguistic features of oral formulaic performance are not greatly in evidence.

HIGH RATE OF SALE AUCTIONS

In contrast to the previous auctions, we turn now to two auction situations in which the rate of sale in lots per minute is very rapid and in which bids are made very rapidly, thus placing pressure on an auctioneer to keep pace with the bidding and the required rate of sale.

Tobacco Auctions of the Southern United States.

Among a number of tobacco auctions, I attended the auctions held in Fuquay-Varina, North Carolina, in early September 1981, one of which was at the Roberts Warehouse. The Roberts tobacco warehouse is typical of the locations for tobacco auctions I have visited. It is a large corrugated iron shed with a timber frame; there is an office along one side. During the weeks of the tobacco harvest, growers from the surrounding area who have contracted with Roberts Warehouse for the sale of their crop bring their loose leaf tobacco into the warehouse wrapped in large squares of cloth. The tobacco is weighed and a ticket indicating the weight and the name of the vendor is placed on top of the pile. The piles are placed on the floor in long rows with a small aisle between each row.

On sale day at the warehouse, the buyers and auctioneer may have already completed sales at another warehouse in the town. It is common for the auctioneer to contract with a number of the warehouses in a town. This may mean disposing of the contents of two warehouses before lunch and two more afterward. When selling tobacco, the auctioneer and his team stand on one side of the pile and the buyers stand on the other. There are a small number of buyers from tobacco companies and one buyer represents a stabilization authority who makes sure that prices do not drop below a predetermined threshold. The buyers shuffle along in single file. In this file each company is in a fixed position; for example, the buyer for the American Tobacco Company leads, followed by Export, R. J. Reynolds, J. P. Taylor and so on. All over the tobacco country of the southern United States, buyers are in the same order by company in every warehouse. As they come to a pile of tobacco some of them will pick up a handful of tobacco, crush it lightly, and sniff it.

At the head of the auctioneer's team is the warehouseman who runs the warehouse. Behind him comes the auctioneer, followed by the auctioneer's assistant. The final person in the team is the person who, after a sale, writes the buyer's name, the purchase price, and the buyer's grading of the tobacco on the ticket taken from the pile. As the two files of people move to each pile of tobacco, the warehouseman calls an opening bid. If this is not accepted, as is often the case, the auctioneer then runs down the scale from that value until he does get a response. Bidding is done by gesture, each arrangement of fingers indicating a number. It is silent and instantaneous in that a number of bidders are bidding at once. Usually, though, a buyer does not make more than one or two bids. The bids are called in ascending order until, at the end of the auction, the buyer is named. This leaves the clerical member of the auctioneer's party to record the sale price and buyer.

Very occasionally the process stops. A buyer might want a pile of tobacco leaves turned over to be sure that the quality of the tobacco is even right through the pile, or there might be a dispute as to the highest bidder. But for the most part the dual procession shuffles past the piles of tobacco without interruption and then rounds the turn into the next row. In the old days, it is reported to me by one informant that some auctioneers would lead the company in a chorus of "Amazing Grace" as they rounded the turn.

Tobacco auctioneers sell a lot about every 5 seconds. This places them at the high end of the pressure scale. The linguistic skills associated with this high pressure are on show at the World Tobacco Auctioning Championships, the first of which I attended in 1981. Typical examples taken from these championships held at Danville, Virginia in the fall of 1981 are the following texts. They are transcripts of recordings provided by Billy Yeargin of Oxford, North Carolina. The duration of each auction is given in brackets at the end.

III.1   Starter's shout: One eighty-one.
Auctioneer: One eighty-one, bid two, two, two, three,
four, four, five, five, bid six, six, eighty-six
dollars, Dibrell. {4 seconds}

IV.1   Starter's shout: One eighty-one.
Auctioneer: Eighty-six dollar bid, seven, I got seven,
all agin you now. Seven dollar bid, seven dollar bid,
Agin Greenville. {5 seconds}

V.1   Starter's shout: Eighty.
Auctioneer: Eighty-five, eighty, ninety, I got ninety
bid, Jenny. {3 seconds}

VI.1   Starter's shout: One eighty-one.
Auctioneer: One eighty-one, five, eighty-six, eighty-six
dollar bid, Dibrell. {3 seconds}

What goes on in the speech of the tobacco auctioneer is described by Bob Cage, himself an experienced tobacco auctioneer and a contestant at the aforementioned auctioning championship:[5]

> We are often asked, "What is all this mumbo-jumbo? What is the auctioneer actually saying as he goes about his business of selling tobacco?" Well, he is rapidly crying the prices bid by the different buyers and the names of the companies these buyers represent with, of course, his own phrases thrown in. For instance, a starter might appraise a pile of tobacco at 38 cents. Then the auctioneer immediately starts his chant at 38 and if two or more buyers bid this tobacco up 'til the final bid is made say by

---

[5]This quotation is a transcript of a tape recording provided by Billy Yeargin of Oxford, North Carolina. It is undated.

Imperial at 45 it would sound like this in slow motion: "38 gi'me nine, nine, 40 will ye? one I got two, two, two, two, make it three now, four, four now, five I got five, forty-five Imperial."

The shout of the starter, the chant of the auctioneer, and the fact that it is scarcely possible to detect the buyers making their bids all provide the atmosphere of a weird ceremonial far removed from the exchange of hard cash. A basket of tobacco weighing around 300 pounds can be knocked out to the highest bidder in a matter of 6 seconds or less. The auctioneer can take bids from perhaps a dozen buyers, adjust his price accordingly, and sell up to about $2,000 worth of tobacco every minute, a feat of salesmanship it might be difficult to equal anywhere.

This description makes it clear that a knowledgeable tobacco auctioneer like Bob Cage is aware of both the ritual context in which tobacco auctioning takes place and the rapid pace of the auction. As he outlined them, the discourse rules of tobacco auctions are, to a large extent, identical to those of the auctions in the previous section. In particular, the discourse structure has most of the same parts. Only the description of the lot is missing. As the buyers are all present, and can see, feel, and smell the tobacco, and the auction is under severe pressure of time, the description of the lot can apparently be dispensed with. The opening bid search is taken care of by the warehouseman's (or starter's) shout. If this shout is not successful in gaining a first bid, then the auctioneer runs down the scale of values from that point until a bid is found and then runs up again until a sale is made. The making of a sale is not indicated by the fall of the gavel but by saying the buyer's name. There is no time for an epilogue. Therefore, the discourse structure rule is the same as for the previous auctions except that the linguistic implementation of the description has been deleted.

What of formulae? The auction quoted by Bob Cage contains a number of bid calling formulae:

1. I got X.
2. X now.
3. X Will ye X+1?
4. X Make it X+1.
5. X Gi'me X+1.

Because Bob Cage is an heir to the tobacco auctioning tradition and himself a practictioner within that tradition, I assume these are formulae of the tradition. However, the auction that Cage used as illustration is more thickly strewn with formulae than the very lean and quite typical texts cited earlier (Transcripts III, V and VI). Only one of the four auctioneers represented there is as free with formulae as the auction example offered by Cage (Transcript IV). The others call the bids with only the following formulae:

1. X bid.
2. I got X bid.

3.   Agin N.

It seems that all tobacco auctioneers use formulae and that they use no freely created novel utterances. What we can conclude is that tobacco auctioneers have a small formula dictionary and that given the speed at which their auctions proceed, they use an even more restricted subset of that already small dictionary.

The tobacco auctioneers' articulation rate ranges from four to five syllables a second up to about eight to 10 syllables in the case of Harry Crisp from Pine Tops, North Carolina, recorded at the First World Tobacco Auctioning Championships. In the following transcript Crisp is slightly slower at the ends of the auction, and at his fastest in the middle.

VII.1   A dollar seventy bi bi eighty dollar eightely eightely
          bee bee bee eightely bee eightely bee eightyfivedollar
          bill now now Virginia   {4.5 seconds}

With such rapid articulation, what is being said becomes severely distorted. Most two-syllable words are reduced to one syllable. Most words come to have simple consonant-plus-vowel syllables. For example, the word *seven* becomes *se* and the word *five* becomes *bi*. Tobacco auction speech shows no hesitation phenomena. Despite the limited vocabulary it is therefore very fluent

All tobacco auctioneers chant, and in a variety of ways. Kuiper and Tillis (1986) suggested that the musical element of this chant is borrowed from southern United States Black musical traditions.[6]

Christchurch Wool Auction

The Christchurch wool auction is conducted once a month almost all year round, with buyers and brokers coming from all over New Zealand and from overseas to buy. All of them are professionals and some form a traveling road show moving from sale to sale. The sale itself is held in what looks like a large lecture theater with tiered rows of seats, every bidder identified by a label. Stock and station (ranch) agencies act as agents for the wool growers, selling the wool from a catalog that indicates its provenance, the quantity, and various measures of its type and quality (e.g., its fineness). Each lot is represented by samples to which the buyers have access at the sale rooms, but the lot itself is in a number of woolsheds at some distance from the sale.

Each stock and station agency in turn sells from its catalog; the auctioneer announces each lot by calling its catalog number and a trial bid. Thereafter, buyers bid verbally, often ending with a period of antiphonal bidding where two buyers

---

[6]The idiosyncratic variation of tobacco auctioneers is a worthy object of research. Many of the wonderful ranges of styles are musically complex. The musicologist Geoffrey Miller has made a start on this kind of study for general auction speech in upstate New York (Miller, 1984).

bid against each other. If the auctioneer senses a brief break in the process, he might repeat the current call. When he senses the bidding is finished, he calls the sale price and the buyer's name. Two sample wool auctions are given in the following transcripts. These transcripts are arranged to show clearly the division of labor among the auctioneer, his bid spotting assistants, and the buyers. The following auctions were recorded by the author at the Seventh Canterbury sale of the 1982–1983 season on March 4, 1983. They are lot numbers 4 and 5.

	Auctioneer	*Assistant(s)*	*Buyers*
VIII.1	Four		
	two ninety		one
			two
			three
VIII.5			four
			five
			six
			seven
			eight
VIII.10			nine
			ten
			one
	three eleven		
	RP		{13 seconds}

	Auctioneer	*Assistant(s)*	*Buyers*
IX.1	Five		
	three seventy	yes	
			eighty
			one
IX.5			two
			three
			four
			five
			six
IX.10			seven
			eight
			nine
			ten
	three ninety		
IX.15	Feltex		one
			two
	two		
	three		
	ninety-two		
	Feltex		{10 seconds}

The rate of sale for wool auction averages under one lot per 10 seconds.

The discourse structure of these auctions is by now familiar. The (reduced) description of the lot is represented by the call of the lot number at the start of the auction, the opening bid search by the auctioneer's first call. However, the bid calling is done mainly by the buyers and there are no formulae. After the sale has been made the auctioneer announces the sale price and buyer's code. All the auctioneer says other than the buyer's name are numbers.

These factors make New Zealand wool sales rather different from other fast auctions because the burden of speech has been passed from the auctioneer to the buyers. The reason for this is clear when the effect of extreme working memory and processing pressure on these auctioneers is analyzed. This is an auction stripped to its essentials. Of all auction sales, the wool auction is thus linguistically the most minimal, demonstrating the bare minimum of speech being used.

Insofar as wool auctioneers speak at all, they are fluent, but that is not saying much when the maximum stretch of speech over which they can be fluent is half a dozen syllables. These syllables are spoken in a monotone, although again, because there are so few syllables, it can hardly be said that wool auctioneers drone.

Properties of High-Pressure Auctions

What makes the auctioning of tobacco and wool similar as far as the cognitive processing of the auctioneers is concerned? They clearly have many of the same processing tasks as auctioneers who sell much more slowly. They must remember where they are in the bidding sequence and so on. One factor that differentiates this group of auctioneers from the real estate auctioneer and the Sotheby's auctioneer is that the rate at which they are expected to sell is much faster. Whereas a house auction may take minutes and an antique auction from about 30 to 90 seconds, a wool or tobaccco auction takes under 10 seconds on average. The rate at which auctioneers are expected to speak is also fast.

Various techniques are employed to ease the burden created by having to perform at speed. In the case of the tobacco auctioneer, the buyers always stand in a single line in the same order of companies, making it easier for the auctioneer to see who is bidding and to know which company the bidder represents. The wool buyers sit in a large room and so visual bid spotting is more difficult for wool auctioneers than for the tobacco auctioneer. Although the physical situation of antique auctioneers is the same as that of wool auctioneers, the high pace of the latter auction apparently does not allow bid spotting and calling to take place at the needed rate. This seems to be the reason why the task of calling the bids has been given to the buyers themselves.

That buyer-called bids are a better division of labor is shown by considering the relative pressure on an individual buyer contrasted with that on the auctioneer. If the bidding were done nonverbally by the wool buyers, the auctioneer and his assistants would need to watch the whole gallery (up to 30 buyers). In addition, the bidding usually covers only a very small range of values, so that if four people were to raise their hands at the same time then the auctioneer would not know how much each was prepared to bid nor would he be able to call the bids in their correct sequence. In the case of the tobacco auctions, with their small gallery of buyers close to the auctioneer, hand signals indicate not just that a bid is being made but the actual value of the bid. In wool auctions, the bidders are sitting too far from the auctioneer and there are too many of them for this to be a possible bidding stategy.

Now compare this division of labor with the system in which the buyers call their bids. Each buyer hears the immediately preceding call and can then decide whether he or she wishes to pay more. There is no need for the buyer to locate the bid in space because it is of little consequence to a buyer who else is bidding, only what value they are bidding at. This enables the auctioneer and his assistants to concentrate on the identity of the final bidder, on calling the numbers from the catalog and calling trial opening bids.

Neither is it possible to slow the auction down. There are many lots to sell and, as the time of the buyers and brokers is valuable, the more quickly the auction is over the better. The press of time is a key traditional feature of these auctions.

A further factor linking fast auctions is that the buyers belong to a closed community, which means it is possible to have very rapid auctioning because everyone knows exactly what is going on. In contrast, in the slow auctions discussed in the previous section, both professional buyers and amateurs are present, making it impossible for speech and selling to be very rapid.

Turning now to the linguistic features of the speech of auctioneers who sell at speed, recall that the discourse of these auctioneers is governed by a subset of the discourse rules used by auctioneers who sell slowly. They use few if any formulae and, if they use formulae at all, these are linguistically quite reduced.

They have an articulation rate that is not only fast but even and in the case of tobacco auctioneers, they chant. Their speech is, to put it differently, highly elliptical, requiring a great deal of inference on the part of the buyers to understand what is said. Because this is a ritual context with which all participants are familiar, everyone knows what the single syllable *se,* uttered by a particular auctioneer in a tobacco auction, might mean (i.e., that the auctioneer is currently seeking a bid of $70 for the current lot in the case where no bid has yet been made or otherwise that the highest current bid is $70). Such speech is very low on redundancy.

Conclusion

The necessity to sell fast and speak fast simultaneously puts pressure on auctioneers in rapid auctions to develop the kind of speech that produces maximum results for minimum effort. The range of choices for doing this is limited. Some form of fixed procedure is necessary for selling at auction. But formulae are almost entirely absent from fast auctions, although there is evidence in the case of tobacco auctioneers that they have a small formula dictionary for various purposes, such as bid calling and hurrying the buyers along. The wool auction is the least verbal of all auctions we have looked at and it could easily be automated, thus becoming a speechless auction system. In fact, this has now happened: Today part of the wool auction in Christchurch is conducted by computer. In the previous examples, the pressures on the wool auctioneer are relieved by having a fully professional bench of buyers who call bids themselves, thus allowing the selling to take place in the minimum time.

The speech of auctioneers who sell in fast auctions therefore shows some of the features of formulaic speech: discourse rules, some elements of abnormal fluency, and droned intonation. The one thing missing is an elaborated incidence of formulae. It seems that formulae are the victim of the increased pressures these auctioneers are under to sell rapidly. So the speech of these auctioneers is not the same as the formulaic performance of play-by-play commentators. Their speech is in some sense minimal, having few if any syntactic constructions.

One factor that likely facilitates this kind of minimal performance is having only professional buyers who do not need to be chivvied, cajoled, aided, or entertained. Buying is their business. They are also experienced auctiongoers, knowing how and when to bid, and what the range of values for the lot is likely to be; they also tend not to be indecisive but to bid when it is required in the auction sequence. So their presence in one sense eases the auctioneer's task, because he can expect such buyers to behave in a largely predictable manner. But their presence also makes for the possibility of very rapid rates of sale with its resulting pressure on the auctioneer's working memory and speech processing capacity. To accommodate this possibility, a rigid lineup is used for the tobacco auctions and buyer-dominated vocalization is used for the wool auctions.

Contrast this with the slower rate of the Sotheby's auction. Why does this kind of sale not move faster? The Sotheby's sale has a largely professional gallery of buyers. In other traditions, such as the wool auction, their presence is associated with, and in part allows for, a fast rate of sale. I suggest that, culturally speaking, rushing headlong through the sale of a valuable antique would be considered indecorous. There is another factor: The monetary value of valuable antiques is not as clear as in the case of primary commodities, such as wool and tobacco, where the range of values is small. Because it is the purpose of an auction to set values, where those values are not within a narrow band, the auction must take the time required for the market to establish an item's value.

As a result of the variety of factors so far mentioned, each auction tradition appears to have its pace governed by a normative metronome setting governed by factors such as decorum and potential value range. The slow-paced auctions traditionally demand a certain experiencing. A Stradivarius or a van Gogh is thus not to be sold at breakneck speed, not just because it takes buyers time to think whether to commit themselves to another massive bid, or because they are not quite sure what the upper boundary on the value of such a lot might be, but because such lots are like fine wine, to be savored, not to be gulped down.

In sum, neither the fast nor the slow auction traditions we have looked at show all of the features of formulaic speech we found for race callers. To find those within auction traditions we must turn to auctioneers who are under a middling amount of pressure. The two traditions we look at to exemplify this are general auctioneers and livestock auctioneers.

MEDIUM RATE OF SALE AUCTIONS

The auctions described in this section appear to place auctioneers under a medium amount of pressure. Again the factors that do this are complex. First, the rate of sale is in the middle range of somewhere between 30 and 90 seconds, giving the auctioneer time to speak more extensively than at the high-pressure auctions. This slower rate of sale allows buyers longer to make up their minds whether to bid. One consequence of this is that the bidding may stall, requiring the auctioneer to attempt to restart the bidding. Second, the gallery of buyers at these auctions is mixed. There are some experienced buyers but also, in many instances, infrequent attenders. Such potential bidders require more attention from the auctioneer; he may need to encourage them to bid and because their bidding styles can be unfamiliar, he may need to see whether they are indeed bidding at any one point. Someone who is a "regular" will normally bid in a consistent manner, for example, by nodding. A novice may nod but not intend that nod to be taken as a bid. All these factors can be assumed to create cognitive processing pressures in that they require the auctioneer to attend to matters other than speaking.

Antique Auctions Conducted by General Auctioneers

Antiques are sold not only at the great auction houses with their wealthy and largely professional buyers, but also in smaller and larger auction rooms in many parts of the English-speaking world by general auctioneers who sell furniture, estates of the deceased, and the like. The pressures on these auctioneers seem to be midway between those of very slow and very fast auctions. The general antique auctioneer must move expeditiously through a large catalog but he does not have the luxury of an educated or professional gallery of buyers. R.G. "Dickie" Bell, one of the two auctioneers whose speech I present in this section, has to tell some of his bidders to put their hands up to bid, and to lead them by indicating that a lot is currently going too cheaply. He is much more overtly required to be a salesman than the Sotheby's auctioneer. Being sold at Sotheby's is sales pitch enough. Bell and Douglas Bilodeau, the other auctioneer featured in this section, must maintain pressure on the buyers; consequently, they use more interpolations and a speedier rhythm while they call bids than the Sotheby's auctioneer.

The pressure of bid spotting is lessened by the fact that Bell wants people to raise their hands and instructs them to do so, whereas Bilodeau has bidders raising numbered paddles to identify themselves and indicate that they are bidding. This decreases some of the pressure on the auctioneer. In this way, Bilodeau has less to do than a Sotheby's auctioneer, who must look for less obvious indications of a bid and locate bidders by their location in the auction hall or their personal features rather than a number that he can plainly read on a paddle.

Douglas Galleries in Deerfield, Massachusetts is operated by Bilodeau. Anyone who enters Douglas Galleries intent on bidding registers with the gallery for the particular sale and is given a bidding paddle. The gallery has a rostrum at the front and next to it a large table for the necessary clerical work. The lots for sale are brought up to the rostrum from behind the auctioneer and held up for the gallery of buyers and spectators to see. Bilodeau is usually assisted by one or two bid spotters who call out when they see a raised paddle. The gallery of buyers and spectators can be quite large, over 100 not being unusual. Many are amateurs, although there are a number of antique dealers amongst them who buy as part of their occupation. For the most part even the amateurs are not novices because attending Douglas Galleries seems to be a local social event where people know they may occasionally pick up a bargain.

The following are transcripts of two of Bilodeau's auctions. These were tape recorded by Geoffrey Miller on December 5, 1980.

X.1   Twenty-seven is an oak medicine cabinet
      oak medicine cabinet.
      Twenty-five dollars for the oak medicine cabinet.
      Twenty-five dollars on it.
X.5   Twenty-five dollars on it.
      Ten dollar bill.
      Ten bid on the oak medicine cabinet fifteen dollars.
      The bid is ten dollars and twelve fifty.
      Twelve fifty on your oak medicine cabinet.
X.10 Twelve fifty.
      Fifteen dollars.
      Fifteen.
      Seventeen fifty.
      Twenty dollars.
X.15 Twenty-two fifty.
      Twenty-two fifty, sir.
      Twenty-five.
      Twenty-two fifty's the bid now twenty-five.
      Twenty-five.
X.20 Sold twenty-two fifty.
      Six-nine.   {28 seconds}

XI.1 Number fifteen
      is a white gold watch.
      I believe the chain
      is fourteen carat white gold.
XI.5 I believe the watch itself is platinum.
      It is set with twenty-six diamonds.
      Twenty-six diamonds
      around the side of the watch.

Very pretty watch.
XI.10   A nice weight to it.
What's your pleasure on the wristwatch?
Five hundred dollars please on the diamond and platinum wristwatch?
Five hundred dollars on it?
I have two hundred dollars and three hundred.
XI.15   The bid is two hundred dollars on the watch
and three hundred dollars.
Three hundred.
The bid is two hundred.
Two fifty.
XI.20   Two fifty.
Two fifty.
It's gold,
platinum,
and diamonds.
XI.25   The bid is two hundred dollars.
Two hundred and fifty dollars.
Two fifty.
Worth that in scrap.
Two fifty.
XI.30   Going
at two hundred dollars.
Two hundred and fifty dollars.
Two fifty.
Any advance?
XI.35   Two fifty.
Two fifty.
(bang)
Sold two hundred dollars.
There's a bid two hundred dollars.   {48 seconds}

At the other end of the world in another village, R. G. "Dickie" Bell of Kaiapoi, near Christchurch, New Zealand, sells antiques and jewelry in a very similar fashion. An old man, who has been auctioning for many years, he wears half-frame spectacles to see the catalog and peers over them at the audience. The gavel rests lightly in his hand. His inventory of formulae is extensive and he uses them with considerable skill as the following transcripts show. These auctions were recorded by the author on April 7, 1982.

XII.1   An eighteen carat gold mounted solitaire diamond ring.
It's a beauty too.
And a very white stone.
Look at the size of it.
XII.5   Nearly three quarters of a carat.

        How much for it?
        Don't know where to start you on this.
        Six hundred?
        Right.
XII.10 Six hundred I've got.
        Six hundred, six hundred, six hundred.
        It's a mighty big diamond here.
        Seven.
        Seven hundred, seven hundred, seven hundred.
XII.15 Seven hundred, seven hundred, seven hundred.
        Seven hundred, seven hu
        This is an investment.
        Seven hundred, seven hundred, seven hundred.
        Seven hundred, seven hundred, seven hundred.
XII.20 Seven fifty.
        I'll take it.
        Seven fifty, seven fifty, seven fifty.
        At seven fifty.
        Are you all done at seven fifty?
XII.25 That lovely solitaire,
        whatever's wrong with that?
        I thought it would have fetched over a thousand.
        Seven fifty.
        All out.
XII.30 Seven fifty.   {53 seconds}

XIII.1 An F.
        An F. Hampton
        That should be T.
        That should be an "n" in your catalog there.
XIII.5 An F. Hampton gents' hunter pocket watch,
        ten-year case,
        and it's a beauty.
        It's a beauty.
        One hundred I've got for it.
XIII.10 One hundred, one hundred, one hundred, one hundred.
        One hundred, one hundred, one hundred.
        One hundred, one hundred.
        At one hundred
        for that lovely pocket watch.
XIII.15 Hunter.
        One ten-year case.
        One hundred, one hundred, one hundred.
        At one hundred.
        Are you all done at one hundred?

XIII.20   Whatever's wrong with that?
          It's a beautiful watch.
          At one hundred.
          A lovely deal on it
          for one hundred.
XIII.25   Any more?
          Well how much do you think it's worth?
          Do you think I'm too high?
          You start it.
          Eighty.
XIII.30   It's a glorious watch.
          Eighty dollars for it.
          Seventy.
          Seventy I've got in two places.
          I took it here first.
XIII.35   Seventy dollars, seventy dollars, seventy dollars.
          Seventy dollars, seventy dollars, seventy dollars.
          Seventy dollars eighty.
          Eighty dollars, eighty dollars, eighty dollars.
          Eighty dollars, eighty dollars.
XIII.40   I'd like my hundred.
          Eighty dollars, eighty dollars, eighty dollars.
          At eighty dollars
          for a lovely watch.
          At eighty dollars
XIII.45   and it's as good a
          in good going order.
          At eighty dollars.
          Ninety.
          Ninety dollars, ninety dollars, ninety dollars.
XIII.50   Still hope.
          Ninety dollars, ninety dollars, ninety dollars.
          A hundred.
          Thank you.
          You've made my day.
XIII.55   A hundred.
          A hundred dollars, a hundred dollars.
          A hundred dollars.
          At a hundred dollars.
          Any more.
XIII.60   You sure?
          Hundred dollars.
          Lady here.   {97 seconds}

Both these auctioneers use the same discourse structure as all the previous auctioneers but unlike the real estate auctioneer and those who work in the polite confines of Sotheby's, they are much more likely to use extensive formulae. Here, for example, is a minidictionary of formulae used by Bell. These formulae are taken from a sample of over 50 auctions conducted by Bell that I have collected.

1. Description of the lot formulae:
    a. Oh, a beauty.
    b. Oh, what a beauty.
    c. It's a beauty. (XII.2, XIII.7)
    d. Isn't that lovely.
    e. There's a nice lot for you.
    f. It's a very nice one, isn't it?
    g. Oh, that's nice.
    h. Oh, what a nice one.
    i. They're very, very nice.
2. First bid search formulae:
    a. How much for that?
    b. How much for the X?
    c. X dollars for it? (XII.6)
    d. X dollars I've got for it. (XIII.9)
    e. X dollars for that.
    f. I've got X dollars for them.
3. Bid calling formulae:
    a. X I've got. (XII.10)
    b. X I've got for it. (XIII.9)
    c. X dollars. (XIII.35)
    d. At X dollars.
4. Bid locators:
    a. That was your bid, Sir.
5. Interpolations:
    a. Put your hand up if I can't see you.
    b. Hold your hand up, that's the idea.
    c. I won't trot you.
    d. This is something good here.
    e. What's wrong?
    f. Thank you, Sir. (XIII.53)
6. Presale formulae
    a. Any more? (XIII.25, 59)
    b. All out. (XII.29)
    c. Are you all out?
    d. Are you all finished?
    e. Are you all finished at X?
    f. Are you all done at X? (XII.24)

Most of what Bilodeau and Bell say is presented formulaically. Even the description of the lot, which may seem so spontaneous to a novice buyer, is usually expressed entirely in descriptive formulae. But there are exceptional circumstances such as the description of an unusual lot for which an auctioneer has no appropriate formulae. Here is Bilodeau describing a set of gold suspenders, an item he claims, plausibly, he has not previously put up at auction. Auctioning formulae are italicized.

XIV.1   Number 16. {3-second pause}
         I have sold a number of items in my, ah, in jury over
         a period of years. This is the first time that I have
         sold a solid gold pair of suspenders. {1-second pause
XIV.5   to allow for audible laughter} *There they are.* A
         pair of gold suspenders, {2-second pause} and they are
         just the bill, if you sort of lean to the left or the
         right , 'coz they are on a little pully. {2-second
         pause} And s, if you ca, don't know where you are
XIV.10   going at night, they are also monogrammed, {1-second
         pause} monogrammed both at the front and the back. {2-
         second pause} A pair of gold suspenders. {3-second
         pause}
         What do you ask for a pair of gold suspenders?

Bilodeau and Bell are both very fluent in the bid calling phase of the auction where they are most formulaic. They are also fluent in the description of the lot. Only occasionally are there pauses, voiced or silent, and the occasional anacoluthon (i.e., a restarting of a sentence or word). In the description of the solid gold pair of suspenders there is one very brief voiced pause and a couple of anacolutha but an uncharacteristically large number of unvoiced pauses. Note too how Bilodeau appears to be in the process of creating a formula for the occasion by the repetition of "a pair of gold suspenders." The unvoiced pausing, anacolutha and creation of a temporary formula are predictable in a context where traditional formulae are not available to allow for the normally greater fluency to appear.

Both these auctioneers speak relatively rapidly and have an even syllable production rate when they are bid calling, but the syllable rate at about four or five syllables a second is not, unlike some tobacco auctioneers at eight plus syllables per second, abnormally fast.

The prosodics of the speech of these two auctioneers is a complicated matter. Both of them drone during some, but not all, of the bid calling. Bilodeau begins to drone on his formula *What's your pleasure on the ....* This formula is droned until he gets to the lot and then there is a fall in pitch on the last stressed syllable of the last word of whatever fills the slot at the formula's end. But although much of the bid calling is droned, there is considerable ornamentation. For example, on a bid calling formula such as *four hundred dollars and four fifty,* the first time the formula

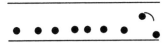

FIG. 3.5. Drone intonation with a high fall tune ornament.

four hundred dollars and four fifty

is said it may all be on a single pitch. But the second time the last word may have a higher pitch on the *fif* syllable and a significantly lower pitch than the tonal center of the drone on the *ty* syllable as in Fig. 3.5. Or it may only lower on the last syllable. There are a number of such variations that ornament the basic drone.

Bell is even more likely to ornament because he is an elderly and very experienced auctioneer who has evolved a large number of bid calling styles, each with its own range of intonational melodies. He may chant the same bid up to 15 times all at a low monotone. Or he may finish a run of four or five with a rising melody on the last stressed syllable. Or he may call each bid with a melody that starts high and finishes low in a kind of dive bombing tune. He also has a bid calling style where he calls each bid twice with the first call's tune starting high and coming down, whereas the second has it starting low and finishing high. He occasionally bid calls in threes, where the three repetitions of the bid are all called at a low monotone but the last has a falling tune at the end. He may call in fours while droning, and the last stressed syllable here may have a higher note followed by a lower note. However, the main bid calling style for both these men is still the low-pitched drone.

In summary, the speech of these two auctioneers has all the features of oral formulaic performance. They use the discourse structure rules of auctioning. They have a large inventory of formulae for each part of the discourse structure. They drone most of the time and they generally have the features of abnormal fluency that characterize the speech of the play-by-play commentator.

Livestock Auctions[7]

It is tempting to attribute the formulaic speech features found in the salesrooms of Bell and Bilodeau to the fact that they are selling interesting items to a mixed audience of semiprofessional and amateur buyers and can therefore play to the gallery. But there is support for regarding the working memory and processing pressure as the more significant factor when we look at the speech of livestock auctioneers. The recordings on which this section is based were made over a period of years from 1977 to 1982. Comparative data have been gathered in Banbury,

---

[7]Much of this section is taken from Kuiper and Haggo (1984). I am grateful to Douglas Haggo for letting me use the work he did on that paper. For a detailed analysis of the prosodic features of livestock auction speech in Canterbury, NZ, see Kuiper and Haggo (1984).

England, Whately, Massachusetts, and Toronto, Canada. The recordings in Canada and England were made by Douglas Haggo in 1981 and 1982.

Livestock sales are a common feature of many primary producing countries. There is little romance in selling livestock to a hard-nosed lot of farmers and professional buyers. That notwithstanding, all the features of formulaic speech are in evidence in the speech of livestock auctioneers. These auctioneers also demonstrate a complex range of additional idiosyncratic properties that makes their speech a useful source of data for investigating how oral traditional material is passed from generation to generation, how it evolves, and how mastery of it is attained (see chap. 4).

The first transcript is from sale days at the Christchurch saleyards. The province of Canterbury on the South Island of New Zealand is a livestock breeding and fattening area. The majority of sheep and cattle raised in the province are bound for export markets and are usually sold on a schedule, the farmer receiving a fixed price per kilogram depending on the type and quality of the beast. For breeding stock, pedigree animals, and the local butchery trade, an auction system of selling is used. Most Canterbury towns and villages have a stockyard consisting of hundreds of pens. Animals trucked from nearby farms are regularly sold at auction in such yards for a variety of purposes. Sales are conducted by stock and station agents, who act on behalf of the vendor of the livestock and advise the farmer on many other matters including when to sell. At the time the recordings for this study were made there were three large companies operating throughout New Zealand, and some smaller firms in various regions. In North Canterbury, there were four firms of agents: Dalgety, Wrightson NMA, NZ Farmers Co-op, and Pyne Gould Guinness.

Sale day begins early on the farms. Beasts coming up for sale have previously been drafted, that is, sorted out from those staying behind. They are picked up early in the morning by stock trucks. (Piglets might be brought in on the farmer's trailer.) At the weekly stock sale in Christchurch, there are different areas of the yards for different kinds of beasts: lambs, breeding ewes, store sheep, store cattle, fat cattle, and so on. Each firm of agents has assigned teams to deal with sheep, cattle, and pigs, and some auctioneers specialize in particular kinds of animal. There is a status hierarchy among the various auctions conducted at a stock sale, ranging from pigs at the bottom, through sheep, to the fat cattle. Often the chief auctioneer of an agency is the person who sells the fat cattle. On the instructions and advice of the auctioneers, the animals are sorted into different grades by stockmen and auctioning then begins in the late morning, usually concluding a few hours later, thus giving the truckers time to take the stock away.

Up to four or five other employees of the company assist the auctioneer. One of these is usually a stockman; the others are either additional auctioneers or junior staff there to spot bidders during the auction and to do the clerical work associated with sales.

The auction takes place in, or by, a pen of beasts being sold. If cattle are being sold, the auctioneer and his assistants usually stand on the rail surrounding the pen, facing the bench of buyers, who normally stand on a raised walkway on the other side of the pen. With sheep, the auctioneer may stand in a pen of sheep and the buyers stand in the race alongside the pen. During the auction, the auctioneer watches the buyers intently, sometimes to the point of being in a half crouch. This is because all bidding is done nonverbally by such means as pulling on one's collar, scratching one's nose, and other time-honored conventions, although mostly just by nodding. Like the auctioneer, the assistants often look as though they are about to pounce on a buyer, because they too are concentrating on the nonverbal signals of their range of potential bidders. The sale moves from pen to pen instead of the lots being brought to the buyers, as is the case in many auction systems such as the Whately auction described at the beginning of this chapter.

In these livestock auctions the description of the lot normally mentions how many beasts are up for auction and where they come from, sometimes by referring to the vendor, sometimes the farm, sometimes the district. Following these two more or less essential items, there may be a string of other descriptive categories, such as the color of the coat or wool, the weight, presale preparation, and so on.

The first bid search is performed by asking for initial bids, with the price the auctioneer thinks the lot will fetch per beast being stated as a trial first bid, a technique we have already seen in other auction traditions. For example, he might say, "Who will give me twenty-three dollars straight out for them?" The first bid might then be taken at $19 and work back up to around the $23 mark. Bidding proceeds by fixed steps. In the case of sheep, the set increment is 20 cents. At a late point in the bidding, the auctioneer may move to change the bidding to half the fixed step. Quite often the bidding stalls, and the auctioneer signals that he may knock down the lot at any time. This is done through the use of specific formulae, such as *right, last call,* or through the use of an intonational tune where the interval is consistently a minor third, especially between the middle and final sections. The lyric is almost always an amount, the last bid (see Fig. 3.6.).

The jump up always follows the first word of the amount. The drop in pitch comes immediately before the last word, and there are no pitch changes other than these steps. Stock auctions do not have the traditional *going once, going twice* routine but use these other presale signals.

In the case of New Zealand livestock auctions, beasts are not sold by weight but by head.[8] This differs from North America, where beasts are weighed, which takes some of the guesswork out of appraisal for both the auctioneer who must call an opening bid and for the buyers.

Making a sale is signaled by the "fall of the hammer," although this may be either the auctioneer's order book, which is slapped down in the palm of his ample hand, or his herding stick, banged on the rail of the pen. Following the making of

---

[8]Since the research on which this section is based was completed, fat cattle have begun being auctioned by weight in Christchurch.

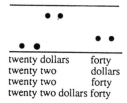

twenty dollars	forty
twenty two	dollars
twenty two	forty
twenty two dollars forty	

FIG. 3.6. Presale intonation melody for a number of bid calls.

a sale, the auctioneer may state the buyer's name or the sale price or both. He may also address the buyer or vendor personally. He then moves on to the next pen where the process is repeated.

In the first transcript that illustrates this auctioning tradition, the auctioneer is Alistair Hopkinson of Pyne Gould Guinness. The auction is a straighforward one in that the auctioneer gets bids at about the optimal rate, that is, there is a bid for each bid call with no delay before the next bid. The lot also fetches the expected price. Hopkinson also shows a concern for the underbidder, the person who has the next lowest bid. Auctioneers are often solicitous for the underbidder because without an underbidder the auction would not have come as far as it has. He tells the underbidder that he is prepared to move from bidding by full increments to bidding by half increments to help the underbidder, and the underbidder responds by making a couple more bids, which pushes the price up a little further. Being solicitous of the welfare of the underbidder is, of course, a way of eliciting further bids and thus raising the sale price. This first livestock auction was recorded in December 1979.

XV.1   I'm not going to beat about the bush.
        These are D. S. Kennedy's cattle from the Oaro on the way to Kaikoura.
        They're off the hill.
        They're particularly well grown.
XV.5   I'm not going to beat about the bush.
        You can all be in the party.
        Got seventy-six dollars for em.
        So you can all have a go.
        Eight.
XV.10   Nine.
        Eighty-one.
        Eighty-two are gone.
        Eighty-three.
        Four.
XV.15   Eighty-five.
        Eighty-five.
        The bidder across there at the main side.
        Eighty-six.
        All right you can all be in the party.

XV.20 Eight-six.
       You can all be.
       Eight.
       Nine.
       Bidder's there, sir. [indistinct].
XV.25 Ninety.
       How are we going, Tommy?
       I've got ninety only for them.
       Right, well I'm going to sell them.
       Right, last call.
XV.30 They're took out at ninety dollars.
       Only got [indistinct]
       One.
       Two.
       Three.
XV.35 Four.
       Five.
       Six.
       I'm going to take a half.
       I'll treat you this time.
XV.40 Now I'm not going to muck about without appealing to you.
       You've been with me all the way.
       Sorry to dwell.
       Ninety-six fifty.
       I'm giving you time.
XV.45 Ninety-seven, half.
       Here's a no, sir.
       Ninety-seven fifty, to the bidder in the back row.   {61 seconds}

The second transcript is of Fred Fowler, then an auctioneer with Dalgety. It illustrates Fred Fowler working with the other men in his team in small dialogues. The recording was made at the same special December sale as that of the previous transcript.

XVI.1 About turn buyers. We'll make a start on this round here.
       Come on the buyers round the corner please.
       Come on buyers. We'll carry on here with the sale.
       All right buyers in this pen being 1579 on account of Mr. D. M. Grant from
           Ahuriri
XVI.5 there are 11 of those Hereford Simmenthal cross steers there
       and they're autumn born those calves.
       They've got a ton of size and length.
       Up they go.
       How much for 'm?
XVI.10 Sixty dollars too for those.
       Sixty dollars.

{Assistant: Fifty.}
I'll go with you, John.
At fifty one.
XVI.15 At fifty-one dollars.
At two.
At fifty-two dollars.
At fifty-two, fifty-two.
Come on, come on.
XVI.20 Look at the stretch.
Fifty-two, two and fifty.
At fifty-two, fifty-two.
Three.
Four.
XVI.25 At fifty-four dollars.
At fifty-four.
Five.
Six.
At fifty-six.
XVI.30 At fifty-six, fifty-six.
Look at
Seven.
Look at the stretch in those in those cattle.
Fifty-seven dollars, seven and fifty.
XVI.35 At fifty-seven, fifty-seven.
{Assistant: Very popular with the local trade butchers.}
They certainly are, John.
Fifty-seven dollars.
Fifty-seven I got.
XVI.40 At fifty-seven, fifty-seven.
{Assistant: Take a half, Fred?}
I'll take a half, Paul.
Fifty-seven.
Half.
XVI.45 Eight.
Half.
Nine.
Half.
Sixty.
XVI.50 At sixty dollars, sixty dollars.
Half.
One.
Sixty-one.
I'll market those cattle.
XVI.55 Half.

Two.
Half.
Three.
Four.
XVI.60 Sixty-four dollars.
Half
Five.
Six.
Seven.
XVI.65 Eight.
Sixty-eight.
I'll sell them now.
Sixty-eight dollars.
Nine.
XVI.70 Now on the counter.
Sixty-nine dollars.
Sixty-nine dollars.
Thank you.
Round this way the disappointed.   {95 seconds}

Stock auctions exhibit the discourse structure of all the other auction systems so far described. However, the discourse grammar of livestock auction speech contains additional rules. For example, unless the provenance is the same as that of the previous pen being sold, the description of the lot always includes the number of beasts for sale and where they come from. The process of moving from bidding by whole denominations to bidding by halves is also a special subrule. The discourse structure rules for livestock auctions in North Canterbury can therefore be given in Fig. 3.7 and can be seen as a variation on the structure of other auctioneers' discourse.

As with the speech of general auctioneers each major phase of the auction contains different formulae. A full dictionary would contain many formulae for

R1 auction ---> description + opening bid search + bid calling + sale + (epilogue)

R2 description ---> [provenance + number] +[(history) + (preparation) + (potential) +

...]

R3 bid calling ---> bid call + n x (bid call + (interpolation)) + (presale) + m x (bid call)

+ (interpolation) + (presale)) + o x (bid by half + (interpolation) +

(presale))

() brackets represent optional choices, [] brackets represent free order sequences.

FIG. 3.7. Discourse structure rules for North Canterbury livestock auctions.

each auctioneer; the following minidictionary is again just a sample.[9] A few of these formulae, such as *on account of,* are used in other auction traditions, but most are unique to livestock auctioning. The dictionary also appears to be somewhat more differentiated than in other auction traditions in that there are subsets of formulae, for example, dealing with particular aspects of the lot description.

1. Sale opening formulae:
    i. Right oh, buyers.
    ii. There we are.
    iii. There they are.
2. Description of the lot formulae:
    a. Provenance
        i.   the property of X from Y
        ii. on account of X   (XVI.4)
        iii. the X sheep/cattle/calves
    b. Number
        i.   There's X in that pen.
        ii. There's X in number.
        iii. There's X in the line.
        iv. There's X of Y there.
    c. History
        i.   The X have been coming here since the year dot.
        ii. You know 'em of old.
3. Bid calling formulae:
    a. Start of bid calling
        i.   I'm under way.
    b. Bid calls
        ii. X I'm bid.
        iii. At X dollars.   (XVI.15)
        iv. X dollars bid.
        v.   X I'm bid.
             X I've got.
        vi. At X dollars.   (XVI.50)
             X dollars.
4. Bid locators:
    i. How's your man?
    ii. Agin your man.
    iii. It's against you, Sir.
    iv. The bid is on your call.
5. Bidding by halves:

[9]The source for these formulae is a corpus of over 100 auctions recorded and in many cases transcribed by the author and his associates from 1977 to 1982. A larger dictionary of North Canterbury livestock auction formulae is contained in Kuiper (1994).

       i. I'll take a half to move.

      ii. I'll take a half that's in the crowd.

     iii. I'll take your half. (XVI.42)

     iv. Have I got a fifty center anywhere?

  6.   Personal address interpolations:

       i. You've come to buy those X.

      ii. You're alright, boss.

     iii. Will you now, Sir?

     iv. Sure you won't, Sir?

      v. We'll sell without you.

  7.   Refer to vendor:

       i. Where's the boss?

      ii. Do I sell 'em?

     iii. On the market, are they?

     iv. Are they on the market?

  8.   Presale formulae:

       i. Last call.

      ii. All done.

     iii. Any better bids?

     iv. Be quick.

      v. Sell away.

     vi. Right, they're away.

    vii.All over.

  9.   Sale epilogue:

       i. X gets 'em.

      ii. X buys 'em.

     iii. They go to Y.

     iv. You're the winner, Sir.

Note again that each formula fulfills one discourse function only, and a variety of formulae are available to fulfill the same discourse function. In comparing this dictionary with that of the general auctioneers, it is notable that the formulae are generally very short and the overlap between the two dictionaries is relatively small. This would be the case even if a much larger dictionary of each tradition was presented. This suggests that each auction tradition tends to develop its own formulaic inventory while sharing a small common core of formulae.

In livestock auctions three prosodic modes appear, each of them characteristic of a different phase. They are drone, shout, and normal. Basically, *shout mode* consists of a drone intonation in which the first stressed syllable in the tonal phrase is produced more loudly and with a higher pitch than the rest of the phrase. *Drone mode* is the kind of even-pitched speech previously described for race calling. *Normal* is the kind of intonation one gets in everyday speech with the kinds of rises and falls in pitch that one expects there. Auction speech is either drone or nondrone (normal), and drone speech is either with or without shout.

Auction constituents	Basic intonational mode	Drone		Normal
		Without shout	With Shout	
Description		+	-	-
Opening bid search		±	±	-
Bid calling		±	±	±
Interpolation		±	-	+
Presale		-	-	+
Epilogue		-	-	+

+ means "must occur", ± means "may occur," and - means "can't occur".

FIG. 3.8. Prosodic modes and their link with discourse constituents of a livestock auction.

The description of the lot is droned; the bid calling is also droned but is punctuated with the shout; and speech with normal intonation is found when the auctioneer moves out of auctioning as such, for example, in interpolations and the epilogue. In the description, only the drone mode is used. The opening bid search is prosodically transitional between the description and the bid calling, in that both drone and shout are usually employed. All three modes appear during the bid calling, but the shout predominates and is the only mode that always occurs in this phase. Interpolations are for the most part prosodically normal, as is speech after the fall of the hammer. Figure 3.8 depicts the prosodic accompaniments of the various discourse constituents of these auctions.

Livestock auctioneers, as can be seen from the transcripts earlier, show very few signs of normal disfluency. Occasionally, in the early phase of an auction, there may be a syntactic false start. This can also happen in the interpolated asides to buyers and vendors, when the auctioneer moves from the equivalent of play-by-play mode into color mode (see chap. 2). Otherwise, auctioneers exhibit the same fluency as play-by-play commentators. Unlike the auctioneers of slow systems, their speech does not contain pauses and, like the speech of tobacco auctioneers, their speech has a strong tonal center although it is not chanted.

In brief, it seems that the speech of livestock auctioneers is like that of general auctioneers. Both sell at a middling rate of sale (in the region of 30–90 seconds per lot) and may therefore be presumed to be under a middling amount of pressure. Both exhibit all the features of formulaic speech.

CONCLUSION

The occurence of formulaic features in the speech of auctioneers varies according to the pressure on the speaker's working memory and processing capacity, as I predicted when looking at the speech of sports commentators. Where there is little pressure on speakers, features of formulaic speech are not greatly in evidence, as shown by the fact that slow auctions such as those at Sotheby's are not droned, and have a relatively low frequency of occurence of formulae. Auctioneers in these traditions also appear to have a smaller repertoire of formulae. As the pressure on auctioneers increases, formulaic speech features occur with increasing frequency, as shown in the speech of general and livestock auctioneers. However, there is a point at which the pressure becomes so great that the auctioneer can only call numbers, as shown in the speech of the tobacco auctioneer and wool auctioneer. As the pressure increases, various strategies for making things easier are used, such as placing all the buyers in a set order, as in the tobacco auctions.

There is clearly also an interplay between the rate of sale and the professionalism of the buyer gallery. The fastest auctions could only be conducted with professional buyers. Such buyers do not not need much talk to encourage them to participate and thus extreme speed takes over at the expense of speech. This factor, as we have seen in the case of Sotheby's, is not a determining one. Professional buyers allow auctioneers to speed up but they do not force them to do so. On the other hand, amateur buyers do force the auctioneer to slow down.

Auction speech thus clearly shows that as cognitive pressure on an auctioneer increases, his ability to say things in an infinite number of ways decreases until, as in the case of the wool auction, he is left with almost nothing at all to say.

The hypothesis of the previous chapter was that the appearance of formulaic features in speech (discourse rules, formulae, droned or chanted intonation, and consequent abnormal fluency) is the result of processing pressures on speakers. The greater those pressures are, the more in evidence the features of formulaic speech will be. In this chapter, these features have been most strongly evident in the speech of auctioneers under middling pressure, less in evidence in the speech of auctioneers under relatively little pressure, and least in evidence in the speech of the auctioneers under the greatest pressure (where the presence of speech is severely attenuated). These observations are, in part, parallel to those of sports commentators, the commentators of slow sports being close to auctioneers under low pressure and commentators of fast sports being like auctioneers under middling pressure. However, the speech of auctioneers under the greatest pressure disconfirms the hypothesis. Why should this be so? I have suggested that it is because once a certain pressure threshold has been exceeded, speech is reduced to single words or a formula or two selected from a very small dictionary. Auctions like this do not develop extensive formula inventories because they do not need them and could not use them even if they were available given the pressure the auctioneers are under.

So, with the addional explanation that beyond a certain pressure point even the limited resources of formulaic speech are excessive, the hypothesis that processing pressures give rise to formulaic speech features is corroborated by the speech of auctioneers.

4

Oral Formulaic Traditions

In the last two chapters I offered support for the theory that the use of the features of formulaic performance is linguistically a way for speakers to cope with being under pressure from doing things other than speaking. I have also shown that the way resources of formulaic speech are utilized depends on the specific register (Biber & Finegan, 1993) the speaker is using. The specific linguistic resources used for race calling, cricket commentary, and the various kinds of auctions are different. In each register tradition, speakers use that register's own discourse rules, its particular formulae, and its prosodics. These are not created by individual speakers but are part of a tradition to which each sportscaster and auctioneer is an heir. So we can now ask how individual speakers acquire such linguistic resources. Two processes must be involved: the creation and evolution of these resources through time and the acquisition of the resources by individual speakers.

THE ORIGINS AND ACQUISITION OF THE REGISTER OF NEW ZEALAND RACE CALLERS[1]

Race calling is a radio register and as such its origins are recent. Two factors make it difficult to explore its very early days. First, the early radio broadcasters from the 1920s are now either so old they are unable to perform or have died. Second, extensive recordings of early broadcasts are difficult to find. In the case of New Zealand race callers, it is nevertheless possible to reach some interesting conclusions about the origins of the traditional oral resources that race callers today draw on by using a small sample of early recordings.

The first broadcast of a racing commentary was also one of the earliest external radio broadcasts in New Zealand, preceded (appropriately enough for this culture) only by the broadcast of a rugby football match. It was made in June 1926 in Christchurch by Allan Allardice on amateur wireless and was followed in the same year by further meetings broadcast on commercial wireless. The origins of racing

---

[1]A fuller version of this material is contained in Kuiper (1991).

commentary in New Zealand can therefore be precisely fixed with the King's Birthday meeting of the Canterbury Park Trotting Club in Christchurch in June 1926. But the oral tradition of Christchurch race callers did not spring full fledged into being on that date.

How did the features of race calling described in chapter 2 come to exist and then to evolve into their contemporary form? The samples of the calling tradition that I have been able to obtain are tantalizing, first because they commence relatively late in the race and second because there are so few of them. The recordings are of race callers of the New Zealand Trotting Cup and the New Zealand Cup for gallopers, and they were provided by Radio New Zealand. They include two recordings made of Frank Jarrett in 1935, five of Dave Clarkson recorded in 1941, 1945, 1954, 1956, and 1966, and two of Reon Murtha recorded in 1972 and 1987.

To see how the specifics of the oral tradition of race calling in Christchurch have developed, I looked at these early recordings for those features of the call that are largely invariant today.

The discourse structure rules for race calling constructed in chapter 2 seem to have been established by 1935. Frank Jarrett, the caller in Christchurch then, uses the same three rules (Fig. 2.1) as Reon Murtha does today. So this aspect of race calling must have come into being in the early years of wireless broadcasting.

One way in which the use of discourse structure rules has changed concerns the loop formulae. When Jarrett looped using a formula that locates the current position of the field in the race, he used either a race locator or a track locator formula but not both. This contrasts with the contemporary practice of using both a track locator and a race locator formula in that order until very near the end of the race. He also tended to use field locator formulae within the cycle quite frequently. Clarkson in the early calls had a strong preference for race locators as loops but, in the last two races for which there are recordings in the sample, tended to use track locators more often. There is an interesting distinction here between gallops and harness racing. When calling gallops, where the track is much larger, the caller is more likely to call the race location because the field passes indicator pegs of the distance left to run. In harness racing, with its smaller track, it is easy to mention the track location because this changes frequently.

Reon Murtha's practice is generally to place the field by its location on the track at the beginning of the race, in the middle stages to call both the track location and the race location, and at the conclusion of the race only the track location.

We can conclude that the discourse structure rules for race calling were established by 1935 but that their implementation has changed a little over the years.

A second area in which the tradition has changed is the order in which horses are called. The present discourse structure rules require horses to be called in the order in which they come. But syntax of English makes it possible to name horses in the reverse order to that in which they are currently running, for example, *Horse 1 is behind Horse 2*. Such reverse order makes it difficult for the caller in that he must have two horses in view and reverse their order in the syntax. It also creates problems for the hearer who hears horses' names in the reverse order and has to transpose them to get the right order. On those grounds, one would predict that reversals are rare. That is certainly the case, but they do occur in some of the early recordings. Dave Clarkson was the only one of the three callers to use reverse order. There are five reverses in the 1941 call, one each in calls in 1945, 1955, and 1956 and none in a call in 1966. All except one are subject to a special condition: The horse being called in second place has been mentioned earlier as coming in front of the horse that is in first place. In the following example, the first utterance, "Column is four out on the outside of these three and appears to be galloping well," locates the horse named *Column.* The next sentence, "Cardigan is following Column," locates Cardigan in the reverse syntactic order to the order in which the horses are actually running. But, because the first statement has already given Column's position as coming earlier, the reverse order presumably does not create a problematic mismatch.

It seems that the evolution of the call has moved to prevent reverse order sequences, as Reon Murtha does not use them and Dave Clarkson during his career moved to eliminate them.

On this sized sample it is not possible to detail the evolution of specific formulae. However, the formulae used by Frank Jarrett in 1935 are, in many cases, still in use today. The following are examples of formulae used by Jarrett that are still in use by contemporary callers:

- X is in the lead.
- X's gone into the lead.
- X's (closely) followed (now) by Y.
- The leader (now) is X.
- X is wide out.
- X's (in) on the rails.
- X's got clear.
- X's flying down the outside.
- X's X lengths clear of Y.
- X is next.
- Then comes X.
- X's moved up.
- X from Y.
- Then X.
- X is going (up) to challenge Y.
- X lengths away (now) is Y.

There are three areas in which, counterintuitively, contemporary callers have opted for greater syntactic complexity in formulae than would seem to be necessary. Occasionally, callers mention a horse twice in a row. I call this process *doubling* because it often involves the repetition of not just the horse but the whole or part of the previous formula, for example, "Gold Bar still out in front by twelve lengths. Gold Bar by twelve lengths." Doubling is efficient from a speech production perspective because the second mention of the horse does not require that horse be identified in the visual field. But it is less efficient in giving the audience as many passes through the field as possible. However, doubling serves a purpose other than communicative efficiency. Doubling is found in all the commentaries in the sample. In the early commentaries, most cases of doubling were of the leading horse. In the latter part of the sample, all cases of doubling are of the leader, or the horse that is about to become the leader, although it is true that the overall number of doublings reduces over time. So it appears that doubling has come to be a rhetorical device for highlighting the leader at the beginning of the cycle (see Fig. 4.1).

The second instance of complexity over time involves pronominalization (e.g., "Johnny Globe, he pokes his nose in front."). Of the possible noun phrases that could be pronominalized, only a relatively low fraction are and this fraction has decreased over time (see Fig. 4.2). Furthermore, where pronominalization does take place, it has become restricted to the leaders because it involves a second mention of a horse and is thus a kind of doubling. We can see that doubling and pronominalization are syntactic devices that have evolved to their present form in the career of Dave Clarkson (see Figs. 4.1 and 4.2).

Left dislocations are a third case of increased syntactic complexity. Occasionally, callers produce left dislocated structures, for example, "Johnny Globe, he pokes his nose in front." In the early commentaries there are no left dislocated structures (see Fig. 4.3). But when they do appear later they are also

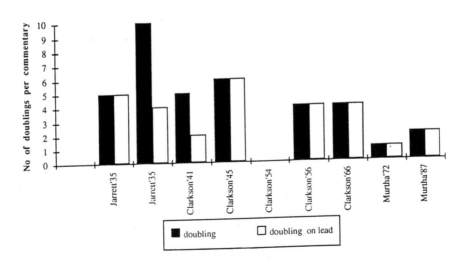

FIG. 4.1. Doubling.

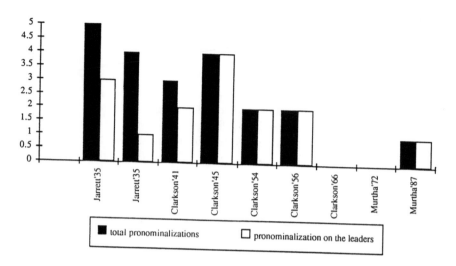

FIG. 4.2. **Pronominalization on the leaders.**

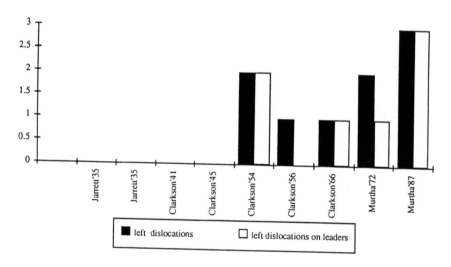

FIG. 4.3. **Left dislocations on the leaders.**

almost exclusively a device for topicalizing the leader, that is, establishing the topic
of the sentence by initial mention of the horse's name. Comparably, Murtha used
greater left dislocation in 1987 than he did 15 years earlier. Clarkson's use spans
over the last 12 years of a 25-year period from 1941 to 1966.

   When I listen to the recordings on which this study is based, one feature of the
development of the tradition stands out starkly and that is the development of the
chanted intonation. The two commentaries by Jarrett (both in 1935) and the first

two by Clarkson (the 1941 and 1945 tracks) are intonationally relatively normal. Jarrett drones a little and has normal fall contours at the end of many of his sentences. Toward the end of the race he does raise the pitch of his voice semitone by semitone, but his highest pitch is reached not at the point at which the horses pass the finishing post but a few seconds earlier. The first Clarkson commentary is almost speechlike with relatively normal intonation. In the second, Clarkson speaks with a mainly level intonation but with a fall tone relatively early in many formulae and, therefore, a rather long following tail. This gives a characteristic dive bomber melody to his 1945 call. But in 1954, Clarkson is chanting in a very similar manner to contemporary callers. At the end of the race, his pitch rises steadily until the race reaches its climax. In the latter commentaries, he is occasionally so excited that his voice breaks on the top notes like that of an inexperienced tenor.

The manifestations of extraordinary fluency also coincide with this period in the evolution of the call (see Fig. 4.4). Jarrett paused quite frequently and hesitated in a normal manner. But after the first years of race calling, Clarkson almost never paused and seldom hesitated in any way. In his 1972 commentary Reon Murtha had one hesitation, but the 1987 one had none and this is the current norm.

We can conclude that by 1935 some of the basic features of race calling were already established. The discourse structure rules had evolved to a form much like their present one and the call was largely formulaic. However, it was not yet chanted and it was relatively normal in its fluency, that is, there was a high proportion of pauses. Many other aspects of the current race calling tradition appear to have evolved during the career of Dave Clarkson. Relatively early in his career, the chant

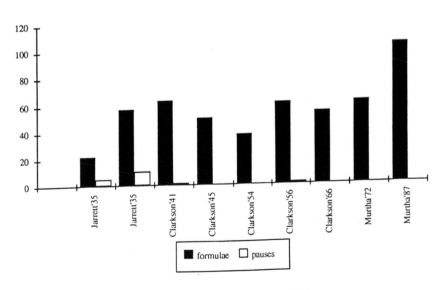

FIG. 4.4. Formulae and pausing.

became mandatory, and the various features for highlighting the leaders such as doubling, left dislocation, and leader pronominalization were established.

This snapshot shows how the parts of the oral tradition to which Reon Murtha was heir arose and evolved. Based on the interview I conducted with him, we can now look at how he acquired it. As a young boy Murtha always had his heart set on becoming a race caller. He described setting up games with improvised objects as horses and calling his own backyard races. After he left school he joined the local radio station, initially as a technician and later as an announcer, but always with the intention of becoming a race caller. At age 19 (in 1960) he called his first race in his home town of Reefton on the West Coast of the South Island of New Zealand. He was initially appointed by the Reefton Jockey Club as its on-course commentator and with that came the possibility of also being the radio commentator. A few years later, the race caller who had covered the race meetings in Greymouth moved and Murtha was appointed by his radio station as the West Coast caller. On the West Coast he called between 10 to 15 race meetings a year. After he had called races for 10 years on the Coast the Christchurch commentator, Dave Clarkson who, as we saw earlier, had been the model for Reon Murtha, changed occupations and Murtha was appointed to the position of race caller for Radio New Zealand in Christchurch.

He now has programs on radio in which he previews race meetings, interviews horse owners and trainers, and gives predictions on possible winners. In this respect, race callers are like ice hockey commentators and other sportscasters in being entertainers as well as informers.[2]

MASTERY OF LIVESTOCK AUCTIONEERING

Can the same approach we have just taken to race calling be taken to auctioning? The answer has to be no. Because oral traditions normally go unrecorded (except those that are broadcast), the only way their history can normally be looked at is through comparative reconstruction. The auctioning tradition, whose current descendents were discussed in the previous chapter, has its origins in England and was exported to the English colonies. For example, one James Wylde was the first auctioneer of livestock to set up in business in Kaiapoi, New Zealand (the town in which R. G. Bell, featured in chap. 3, was also an auctioneer). He was a colonist from England (Hawkins, 1957).

On the basis of historical reconstruction, some of the central features of the English tradition can be suggested. All auction systems in the English tradition appear to share at least one discourse structure rule, the familiar one from the previous chapter: Bid calling is characteristically performed by rising bids with or without fixed increments. There are also two distinct ways of calling bids. In one tradition, only the current highest bid is called, whereas in the other, common in

---

[2]See Kuiper and Haggo (1985) for an account of the oral formulaic performance of ice hockey commentators.

North America as we saw from the transcripts of Douglas Bilodeau, both the current highest bid and the bid currently being sought are called.

There are a number of formulae that must have come to New Zealand from England. I suggest that this is so from the fact that these formulae appear in other parts of the world and other types of auctions. Formulae taken from livestock auction speech in Canada and New Zealand (Haggo & Kuiper, 1985) are the opening bid search *X and go,* the bid calling *X fer 'em,* and the refer-to-vendor *Do I sell 'em?* A formula common to both antique auctions and livestock auctions is the final call *Are you all done?*

These formulae are all discourse-function specific, that is, they function in one and only one of the sections of the discourse structure of auctions. A formula like *Any more bids?* is a bid calling interpolation used when the bidding stalls. *Are you all done?* is used when the same thing happens but very close to the end of the bid calling phase to signal to buyers that a sale is about to be made. One also cannot tell from the particular formula whether it belongs to the tradition of auctioning tobacco or livestock or antiques.

The unusual shout tune is not found in all of the derived traditions but in enough of them to suggest that it may have come from England. For example, in livestock auctions in both New Zealand and Canada a bid calling formula such as *At X dollars* will have the first word articulated with a significantly higher volume and pitch than the rest of the formula and with a sharp staccato delivery. The drone, in some derived traditions, is still speechlike, for example, in livestock auctions. In others, such as the tobacco auctions, it is chanted, that is, has a musical character. Similar chanting exists in a large number of oral traditions other than those of auctioning. Some commentators drone whereas others chant and the two traditions exist alongside each other as stylistic variants. It seems that both drone and shout were likely features of the English auction tradition.

As with race callers, oral traditions among auctioneers are likely passed down from generation to generation and the reflexes of the common source of a tradition remain in the various traditions that have evolved from it. If this is the case, then the oral formulaic performer is the locus for cultural transmission.

The transmission of any oral tradition like auctioning is an apprenticeship system. A novice attaches himself to one or more master performers and learns from them without being explictly taught by them. This is a graduated apprenticeship. The first phase is passive, with a novice spending many hours listening. This is followed by a journeyman period, in which the apprentice auctioneer performs with a limited repertoire and in a limited way, that is, the discourse structure rules and formulae he knows are limited in both number and complexity. The third phase is that of mastery, in which the performer is able to make a personal contribution to the tradition itself.

The livestock auctioneers of North Canterbury come to perform in this way. I have informally observed that stock and station agencies generally recruit their professional staff directly from school. On sale days, a young recruit might be taken to stock sales to help with the yarding of stock and, later, with doing some of the clerical work associated with the auction. In his mid-20s, having experienced many aspects of his company's operations and having attended hundreds of auctions, a young man might be given the opportunity to auction some of the less desirable lots. If he shows promise, he may gradually become a full auctioneer. There is little or no overt training, and auctioneers with whom I have spoken say that an auctioneer is born, not made. It is obvious though that a long period of training of a nondirective sort does precede becoming an auctioneer, and a fully mature auctioneer is usually at least 30. If we look at the transcript of the speech of a younger auctioneer and compare it with the work of master auctioneers, we see the basic functional elements in the former and their exploitation and ornamentation by the latter. The auctioneer in the following transcript is Kerry Shaw of Pyne Gould Guinness, then in his late 20s or early 30s. This auction was recorded on December 12, 1980. He was not a complete novice and had a number of years' experience as an auctioneer. He is now one of the senior auctioneers for his company.

I.1   There you are, gentlemen,
        down from Culverden,
        now, gentlemen,
        the next three pens,
I.5   there's thirteen of those Angus and Angus cross steer calves to go, gentlemen.
        Away we go.
        Young calves, they are.
        Away we go.
        Who'll give me 35?
I.10   Who'll bid a 35 dollar and go there?
        35 and go then?
        28.
        28 dollars.
        I'm under way.
I.15   30, 28, 28, 28, 28 it is.
        At 28.
        All steer calves, you're buying.
        You're buying them at nine.
        30, 30 dollars.
I.20   30 dollar I'm bid.
        30 dollar I got.
        At 30 dollar.
        The bid's below.
        Make no mistake.
I.25   At 30 dollar.
        30 dollar only.
        Alan Haylock, you can have a tickle there.
        30 dollar.

	30 bid.
I.30	30 I got.
	At 30 dollars.
	Last time.
	I'll take a half to move.
	I'll take a half to move.
I.35	They should make close to the 34 dollars, those in that pen, gentlemen.
	Gentlemen, come on.
	30 dollar only.
	30 dollar.
	30 dollar I'm bid.
I.40	At 30 dollar.
	Last time.
	I'll sell them.
	Last time.
	Take a half to move.
I.45	We'll sell away.
	Can't see my vendor about.
	We'll sell.
	Last time.
	30 dollars.
I.50	Last time.
	Be quick.
	30 dollars buys.
	They go below.

This auction is well-crafted. The discourse structure is clear and the transitions from one section to the next clearly signaled. For example, the auction opens with an opening formula, "there you are, gentlemen" (Line I.1), directing the buyers' attention to the lot. The first bid search transition is signaled by "away we go" (Line I.6). Bidding by halves is signaled by "take a half to move" (Lines I.33, 34, 44) and the coming end of the auction by "last time" (Lines I.32, 41, 43, 48, 50). Because the auction fails to reach the price the auctioneer is seeking, he makes several appeals to buyers, including one to a named individual, "Alan Haylock, you can have a tickle there" (Line I.27). He lingers in the presale phase trying to extract more bids because he believes the lot has not reached its expected value. However, there is litle idiosyncrasy. The formulae are short; standard formulae such as these would be used by many auctioneers. Many formulae are repeated. For example, the formula *I'll take a half to move* is used three times (Lines I.33, 34, 44), and the presale formula *last time* five times (Lines I.32, 41, 43, 48, 50). Features such as these make this a good journeyman auction. I should also say that master auctioneers produce similar auctions from time to time but they also have the capacity for a more idiosyncratic and more fluent, less repetitive performance.

Mastery is the stage to which oral formulaic performers in many traditions aspire. It is easier to see mastery being attained in those traditions that have an element of entertainment than in traditions that appear more functional. How does one assess mastery? A master performer in any tradition is almost by definition one whom younger performers use as a model. But there is also an aesthetic element. Even in auctioning traditions, auctioneers and buyers alike can identify the master performers. Some people come to hear such auctioneers just for the pleasure with no intention of buying on this occasion. When questioned, buyers will comment on the best auctioneers' ability to cope with difficult situations, to make humorous reference, and not to be stuck for words. One incident I witnessed shows the latter facility. An auction had stalled because a buyer who had previously been bidding indicated that he no longer wished to do so. The auctioneer whipped around to the buyer and retorted in mock anger, "I suppose you want a quarter," meaning that, because bidding had already moved to bidding by halves, the process could be repeated, moving to quarter increments. This incident created much merriment among the buyers and showed the auctioneer's mastery of his tradition through his ability to use it creatively.

Another example of creativity and mastery is the case of a sale of stud rams in Australia shown on television during which one lot had fetched a world record price. After the record had been exceeded and amidst applause from the gallery, the auctioneer asked the vendor the conventional question as to whether he wanted to sell. This again created great mirth because such a question is normally only asked if the auctioneer is uncertain as to the vendor's wishes.

In tobacco auctioning, the aesthetic dimension was recognized overtly for some years by the existence of a contest that did not test the auctioneer's ability to sell at the highest price but rather his ability to produce the most satisfying performance. These contests were held in Danville, Virginia where the first tobacco was sold at auction in the United States in the mid-19th century. The sponsors of the event went so far as to produce a 45rpm recording of the top contestants at the first championships in 1980.

At least two livestock auctioneers in North Canterbury appear to have attained a high level of mastery of their tradition when the research reported in chapter 3 was conducted. Alistair Hopkinson and Fred Fowler seem to have formulae of their own and to be, at times, extremely creative in their use of them. To see a master livestock auctioneer in action we can look, for example, at the following transcript of an auction conducted by Alistair Hopkinson recorded on February 19, 1979:

II.1   On we go to the Te Tini two tooths.
       There's no footrot on Te Tini.
       And these two tooths have been dipped.
       They're absolutely sound in the feet, gentlemen,
II.5   and they're off the hills straight behind you out there.
       They're absolutely natural condition sheep.
       They're off the tussock.

I'll make you buy it at fifteen twenty,

fifteen forty,

II.10   fifteen dollar forty,

sixty,

eighty,

fifteen eighty.

Come on.

II.15   The Te Tini two tooths,

if you buy 'em you'll be back here next year,

and at fifteen eighty.

They're off the tussock right behind us there, Greg.

You can see the peaks right behind us there.

II.20   Fifteen dollars eighty I got.

Fifteen eighty I'm bid.

At fifteen dollars eighty only.

At fifteen eighty.

Royce Belcher, they'd shift.

II.25   You know where they're from.

Fifteen dollars eighty.

They're damn sweetly woolled

and I've only got fifteen eighty for 'em.

At fifteen dollars eighty.

II.30   Who's going to round it?

Yes or no, Sir?

They'll do all right.

They're absolutely guaranteed in the feet.

There's no footrot up there on them there hills.

II.35   And I got fifteen eighty for 'em.

At fifteen dollars eighty.

Is that a bid?

Yes or no?

That's the cheapest we've sold today, Bill.

II.40   Bar none.

Come on there.

At fifteen dollars eighty.

At fifteen eighty.

Now where have all the buyers gone?

II.45   Has the wind blown them away?

For fifteen dollars eighty.

What do you think, Sir?

Going to go?

Can't go?

II.50   Well, I'll tell you, they'll do well with you.

Royce, is that a bid?

> Yes, or no at fifteen dollars eighty.
> What do you think, Peter?
> On the market?
> II.55   It's a damn poor sale at fifteen dollars eighty.
> Last call.
> Fifteen dollars eighty, right there.
> Thank you.

There are a number of instances of creativity in this auction. First, Hopkinson makes use of the location of the sale in the Amberley sale yards and the clarity of the day; this permits the bench of buyers to see the distant Southern Alps that the auctioneer and his assistant have behind them. He is required by the discourse structure to give the provenance of the sheep and finds a new and appropriate way to do so. He does so on a number of occasions, pointing again and again to the faraway hills (Lines II.5, 18, 19, 34). There are two reasons for this, the main one being that hill country sheep farms generally do not have footrot. But sheep from hill country farms also fatten well on the flat.

Having mentioned the hills, Hopkinson interpolates into the auction a cut-down version of *There's gold in them thar hills* (Line I.34) to point buyers again to the place that the sheep have come from. He also gains an association from the use of this quotation in that the sheep are equated with gold; in this case, it is not metallic gold that has come from "them there hills," but the golden fleeces on the backs of the sheep, a useful equation for someone who is finding difficulty selling a commodity.

Then there are the personal addresses to Royce Belcher (Lines II.24, 51). Such personal addresses are not uncommon but they are not couched in formulae that are part of the tradition of livestock auctioneers. In these two addresses to Royce Belcher, Hoppy (as he is known to most of the auctioneering fraternity in North Canterbury) shifts from the formal mode of address, calling the buyers "gentlemen" to referring one of them by his given name to put greater pressure on him to bid. Others addressed in person are either assistants (Greg and Bill) or the vendor (Peter). Again, the use of these given names is not formulaic.

Then there is reference to the wind (Line II.45). The sale is held in February when the characteristic Canterbury föhn winds blow from the mountains across the plains. The buyers are standing with the dry, dusty wind blowing in their faces, and Hopkinson blames the wind for the lack of bids, again making use of the specifics of the situation to give color to the auction.

The sale seems to be punctuated with these moments of creativity when the auctioneer moves into color mode in order to liven up the sale and exhort the buyers by means beyond the narrow confines of the basic tradition. Each such moment is tailored to particular exigencies of this one sale. The capacity to do this makes a performer a master.

One fact about mastery needs to be emphasized in conclusion. It is difficult to judge mastery unless one is reasonably familiar with a tradition. Only then is it possible to tell what aspects of a particular performer's speech are genuinely creative.

I alluded in chapter 1 to performances that Bauman (1986) referred to as having "the essence of spoken artistry" (p. 3). All formulaic speakers partake of this essence in that they are steeped in a tradition that makes performance possible. In those speakers who have reached mastery in a formulaic tradition this is manifest. It is perceived by the audience members, who can list the master performers, and in some cases, have described to me what it is about master performers that makes them such. Apprentices and journeymen within a tradition too have often been able to explain in discussion with me something of what it is that makes master performers the ones they have modeled themselves on. Master performers, in their turn, know who they took as their model performer(s).

GENDER AND ORAL TRADITIONS

All the oral traditions that have been looked at so far are dominated by male performers. There appear to be no women performing as tobacco auctioneers, or stock and station agents in New Zealand. There are no women race callers, as there were no female performers of heroic poems in Yugoslavia.[3]

The exclusion of women from many formulaic traditions is a complex issue. It is not a universal. There are a number of successful women auctioneers in upstate New York.[4] Women play significant roles in many oral traditions, such as the composition and performance of waiata (songs) in traditional Maori society. However, they are excluded from the performance of formal Maori marae oratory called whaikorero in most, but not all, tribal areas in New Zealand (Salmond, 1975).

Women's exclusion from some of the traditions we have discussed earlier might therefore be seen as a feature of these traditions.

So what is it in these particular traditions that makes them gender linked? One factor is that they appear to be traditions begun by men. The tradition of Canterbury race callers was begun by and transmitted to men, so they became the models for later commentators. It is difficult for a woman to break into such a tradition for two reasons. First, there is the problem of a woman attaching herself to a man as apprentice, a difficulty in any trade but even moreso when long periods of unpaid apprenticeship are involved.[5] Second, audiences become accustomed to hearing men as performers in a tradition and thus women performers have to break audience expectations in order to become accepted.

It is possible to break into some oral traditions by serving in an adjunct capacity, for example, as color commentator. In a relatively loose tradition, such as that of

---

[3]It is an interesting feature of the scholarship in the field that this fact is seldom commented on.

[4]I am grateful to Geoffrey Miller of Kingston, New York, for drawing this to my attention and providing an audiotape of one important woman auctioneer, Dorothy Knapp, for me to listen to.

[5]See Kuiper (1986) for an account of some of the difficulties attendant on women being apprenticed to men in male-dominated trades.

cricket commentator, one woman has become a color commentator in Canterbury, New Zealand. She is Lesley Murdoch, who has excellent credentials as a sportsperson, having been captain of the New Zealand women's cricket team, a former member of the New Zealand women's field hockey team, and currently an umpire of women's hockey at the international level. There is no doubt to those listening that she knows what she is talking about. But she has not become a play-by-play commentator and it remains to be seen whether she will break into the play-by-play tradition.

Women have occasionally become antique auctioneers possibly because antique auctions have, or are seen to have, lesser pressure and require expertise outside the auction arena in appraisal and organization, which women can acquire without initially being auctioneers. For example, Christina Stachurski spent a year auctioning occasionally for R.G. Bell, in Kaiapoi, but no longer does so. Geoffrey Miller (1984) described the auctioning of Dorothy Knapp of West Nyack, New York, who has her own auction rooms. Women appear to be absent from the primary commodity markets.

A further factor in many cases is that the cultural niche in which the oral formulaic tradition is practiced is male dominated. The coffee houses where Yugoslav oral poets perform are closed to women (Lord, 1960). In the livestock sale yards of New Zealand, women occasionally bid if they are farmers in their own right but the large majority of those actively involved are men. The sports where men are commentators are also largely male dominated. This makes it difficult for women to become major participants.

There may be an even more broadly based explanation than the local character of oral traditions. Michelle Rosaldo (1980) suggested:

> That in all human societies sexual asymmetry might be seen to correspond to a rough institutional division between domestic and public spheres of activity, the one built around reproduction, affective, and familial bonds, and, particularly constraining to women; the other, providing for collectivity, jural order, and social cooperation, organised primarily by men. (p. 397)

Because all the oral traditions we have looked at provide for performances that belong primarily in the public rather than the domestic domain, it is not surprising that they have been evolved primarily by and for men.

CONCLUSION

We can conclude that oral traditions are significant cultural artifacts passed down over many generations by an apprenticeship system allowing for cultural continuity and cultural change, for both tradition and individual talent. The primary linguistic resource of these traditions is the inventory of formulae, each of which is related to a particular discourse task. Such formulae are adapted over time, and the inventory added to particularly by master performers. A mature oral tradition thus provides a lexicon that constitutes a finite but adaptable set of linguistic resources; it allows speakers to speak fluently in real time without needing to make up entirely novel utterances to fit every situation. Instead, each formula provides the nucleus of an appropriate utterance for a routine context with which a speaker must deal.

5

Formulaic and Ordinary Speech

WHAT CAUSES SPEAKERS TO USE FORMULAIC SPEECH?

The previous chapters have made a case for supposing that a reduction of linguistic resources in the form of discourse rules, formulae, and stylized prosodics is necessary when speakers are under particular kinds of processing and working memory pressure. Oral formulaic performance provides these reduced linguistic resources and thus allows speakers to deal with processing pressure. But it could be that even without such pressure, when performing routine tasks speakers would over time evolve formulaic traditions to accomplish their speech tasks. There is ample evidence to suggest that this happens (Abrahams, 1970, 1972; Coulmas, 1979, 1981; Edwards & Sienkewicz, 1990; Ferguson, 1976; Rosenberg, 1970). Let us suppose that it happens and ask why. Bauman's (1975) framework for examining performance, which I described in chapter 1, suggests that performance should be examined textually, contextually, and socially. The burden of the previous chapters is that, textually speaking, formulaic performance cuts down the speaker's options. In doing so, it also cuts down the hearer's or audience's options. So we might ask if it is possible that some features of formulaic speech could be resorted to purely in order to cut down the options for the audience. Clearly hearers also have processing tasks to do in extracting what the speaker has said from a speech signal. It may be that restricting what a speaker hears to a formulaic subset of the possible assists hearers.

Formulaic Speech for the Hearer: Weather Forecasting

Hickey (1991) investigated a kind of speech that shows that some of the features of formulaic performance may appear when what the speaker says is scripted and the tradition is entirely a written one.[1] In such circumstances it is not because of working memory pressure that the people who write the scripts use formulaic textual features. They are at no time under working memory pressure, as they do not compose their texts orally and then commit them to memory. (See Finnegan, 1981, for a case of this.) Instead they write and then read their forecast scripts on the radio or television. So, in the speech of broadcast weather forecasts, it appears that the speech routines are created in order to cut down the options for the hearer's benefit.

The weather forecasts in New Zealand on which Hickey's research is based all originated with the forecasts of the New Zealand Meteorological Office, colloquially known as the Met Office. The National forecast from the Met Office gives the weather for the whole country in a standard form. The standard form uses a set of discourse structure rules that ensures that the order in which the weather information is mentioned is always the same. An initial general synopsis is followed by district forecasts. The general synopsis always has the various items of weather information given in the same order. The order in which the district forecasts come is also always the same. Within each district forecast, weather information relating to matters such as precipitation, cloud cover, and temperature is always in the same order.

Forecasters also choose from a set of formulae for each different aspect of the weather. For example, in the general synopsis, a forecaster might wish to describe the properties of a front or a pressure system. This is done by formulae such as *a stationary anticyclone* or *a slow-moving front.* Movement or otherwise is indicated by a finite set of verbs, such as *is located* or *extends.* Location and direction are also indicated by formulae, for example, *over New Zealand, onto the South Island.* Such fragments form parts of finite state systems of the kind that will, by now, be familiar.

The relative stability of these forecasts must be contrasted with the weather itself, which does not come in a fixed order. At one and the same time, rain may fall, the temperature may be at a particular level, there may be a certain amount of wind from a particular direction, and there may be a certain amount of cloud cover. Furthermore, the geographical regions do not come in a fixed order. Because this is so, weather forecasting would require high amounts of attention on the part of the hearer if each synoptic situation ordered the description of the weather in a different way. Hearers would also have to pay close attention if they could not rely on their region being mentioned in the same place in the sequence.

It can be seen that the need to create speech that is easy for an audience to process leads to some of the features of formulaic speech being evident in weather forecasting. Weather forecasting cuts down the options for the hearer, but not as radically as the speech of the race caller does for his audience. Weather forecasting is not droned and, in their interpolations, forecasters in some media provide for the short, less predictable interludes that auctioneers of medium-pressure auction systems also allow themselves.

---

[1]Hickey's findings are supported by the computational work of Mitkov (1991).

Sociocultural Factors in Formulaic Speech

On the basis of the discussion so far I conclude that, because it is necessary in some cases and desirable in others, to cut down the linguistic options for both speakers and hearers, speakers often resort to formulaic speech in routine contexts. Such psychological factors are essentially concerned with individual human memory and processing capacities. They therefore fit into Bauman's contextual area because they have to do with the immediate context of individual speakers and their audience taken as individuals.

Bauman's framework suggests that a third area, the sociocultural, also needs to be taken into account. Societies and cultures provide a dynamic, evolving but fundamentally stable social environment within which human beings act and make sense of their own and others' actions. It is therefore one of the functions of societies and cultures to limit the options humans have as to how they behave. In theory, actions in a social setting might be performed in innumerable ways and cross-cultural ethnography shows just how variously humans act in living as members of social groups. However, within a social group there are limits on how things can be done in a socially sanctioned way, and all societies have ways of dealing with those who act outside socially sanctioned rules. Because speech is a social act, societies sanction some forms of it and not others. We might therefore expect formulae and discourse structure rules in situations where their use is not forced just by psychological factors, but where it is determined by the sociocultural context.

Here are four examples to begin with. They are the opening examples used by Austin (1976) in his discussion of performatives. Performatives are utterances, the saying of which constitutes a social act, a way of, as Austin put it, doing things with words:

1. "I do (sc. take this woman to be my lawful wedded wife)"—as uttered in the course of the wedding ceremony.
2. "I name this ship the *Queen Elizabeth*"as uttered when smashing the bottle against the stem.
3. "I give and bequeath my watch to my brother"—as occurring in a will.
4. "I bet you sixpence it will rain tomorrow."

These expressions have particular conditions of use, a specific context outside of the act of speaking itself within which they may be felicitously and appropriately uttered. What Austin did not note (because it has nothing to do with his discussion) is that these expressions are themselves relatively fixed. It is not just changes in their social contexts that make saying these words socially inappropriate or infelicitous. Even minor changes in the way such performative acts are expressed make them opaque or infelicitous, as Pawley and Syder (1983) pointed out in the case of marriage proposals. If one says in the first context, "It is my wish to concur," then something very odd has been said, and one wonders if the marriage ceremony could or would continue. It happens in most parts of English-speaking culture that

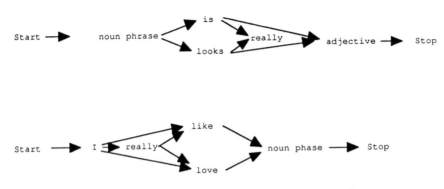

FIG. 5.1. Two American English compliment formulae.

what one says conventionally in this context is "I do" and nothing else. In the second case, if one says, "I give this ship the name *Queen Elizabeth,*" again something odd has been said. Notice that in neither case is there anything odd about the sentence as such. Its content is no more or less appropriate for the purpose than the standard formula. But there is something odd about uttering it in the context in which one would normally use Austin's performative utterances. It is possible, in each case, to think of numerous other ways of "saying the same thing" that would not be regarded socially as saying the same thing. So it seems that there are many performative expressions that qualify as formulae on the grounds that they are relatively fixed expressions which have standard conditions of use within a speech community.

The range of formulae occuring outside the kind of restricted oral formulaic varieties of earlier chapters does not finish with performatives. Greetings, apologies, compliments, and meal openings are typical examples of social acts for which languages will have routine formulae. Such formulae have many of the same properties that they have in the speech of auctioneers and sports commentators, specifically, they are indexed for their social role.

A simple example is the way one is greeted at the supermarket. Flindall (1991) looked at the way in which checkout operators greet the supermarket's customers. Not surprisingly, almost all the greetings are formulae. Why greet customers at the checkout with a routine greeting formula? Because the relationship between most customers and most checkout operators in a supermarket is neither deeply personal nor of long standing, but casual and momentary, the least objectionable way to greet someone with whom one has such a relationship is with an entirely predictable greeting. Because most of the rest of one's relationship with a checkout operator is routine, the greeting one receives is similarly routine.

A similar social act is that of complimenting someone. In a study by Manes and Wolfson (1981), it appeared that virtually all compliments are formulae. Two typical formulae are found in Fig. 5.1.[2]

---

[2]These diagrams are mine, based on Manes and Wolfson's data.

When one compliments someone, as Manes and Wolfson (1981) pointed out, one expresses solidarity with him or her. Using a formula minimizes "potential interference with the expression of solidarity" (p. 117). It also makes "compliments readily identifiable in any context" (p. 117). The reason for this is that the formula is in the dictionary of speakers of, in this case, American English, and it is therefore a familiar expression for the purpose of complimenting people. By contrast, if a speaker were to make up a new expresssion for complimenting someone on the purchase of, say, a new suit, such as *My mother would be grateful to see your suit,* the hearer would be much harder put to identify this as a compliment. This is because the hearer would have to infer that it was meant as a compliment whereas, in the case of a formula such as *I like your suit,* they would know that it is a compliment by convention.[3]

There is nothing inherent in the content of either sentence that makes it particularly apt as a compliment. It could easily follow that, if the speaker's mother were grateful to see the suit, then it must be a nice suit and therefore that the speaker is complimenting the hearer on it. It is equally possible, as in fact is the case in some Polynesian cultures, that uttering the English compliment formula is an indirect request to have possession of the suit.

The social contexts within which formulae are the preferred way to speak extend beyond these small-scale situations to large-scale stretches of discourse. Speech at meetings contains many formulae. So do court proceedings and medical interviews. It seems that very many of the things we do socially with words are not, in fact, done with individual words. They could be done with words but they are actually done, most of the time, with formulae.

That being so, we would expect changes in the social order to be accompanied by changes in the formula inventory. Ji, Kuiper, and Shu (1990) showed that during the Cultural Revolution in the People's Republic of China some formulae that had been used in the past ceased to be used. New formulae came into being and other formulae underwent either internal changes or changes in their conditions of use. For example, traditionally in China, students in school had to show their respect for their teacher by uttering a particular formula at the beginning of the day. However, during the Cultural Revolution, teachers were to be regarded as class enemies and thus not worthy of respect. So, in the place of the morning respect formula, the class monitor would lead all the students and the teacher in a revolutionary greeting that paid homage to Chairman Mao Tse Tung. In this case, and every other examined by Ji, Kuiper, and Shu, changes in the formulae themselves or in their conventional conditions of use were connected with the changed political and social circumstances created by the Cultural Revolution.

The effects of lexicalizing particular expressions as formulae can have effects beyond the immediate context to illuminate general socialization patterns. Kuiper (1990) examined the formulae used by two male sports groups: one a rugby football team, the other a recreational volleyball squad. The rugby players create solidarity

[3]Because it is a conventional compliment it can be used sarcastically.

through their use of a set of formulae whereby players on the same team denigrate each other. These formulae are derogatory forms of address and nicknames, such as *cunt, wanker,* and *shitface.* The other group uses a series of formulae to support one another, apparently because the game is not played competitively and none of the players are particularly good at it. For example, if a player serves out of court, members of his team will say *on the line.* Everyone knows the ball was served out but the player who has served it out is being verbally supported by his teammates.

These two different ways of approaching those with whom one plays a game appear to be the result of different ways of seeing one's fellow players. They may also promote different ways of seeing one's fellows. It may be that this in turn plays a role in the ways in which male socialization takes place and the tenor of relationships among men that is likely.

All these studies show that whereas many formulae have the property of being indexed to discourse structure rules, others are indexed to particular social tasks in which there are no discourse structure rules as such.

If such observations about the use of formulae in speech are generalized, then it should be possible to turn these findings around so that observations of the formulaic inventory of a social group become a possible way to see some aspects of the group's social order more clearly. This was suggested by Herdt (1980):

> Idioms ... set up shared frames for perception, culturally transmitted boundaries with which individuals tacitly recognise or ignore patterns of phenomena. In this way formulae are a social vocabulary to which native members of a culture have access. (p. 197)

This echoes the early linguist Edward Sapir (Mandelbaum, 1958), who wrote that "it is the vocabulary of a language that most clearly reflects the physical and social environment of its speakers" (p. 90). I have shown that this is particularly so of a speaker's and a society's formulaic vocabulary with its conventional indexing to sociocultural tasks and events. Each social event described in the previous chapters, be it an auction or a sporting event, exists conventionally, in part, in the formulaic vocabulary of its own tradition.

Before leaving the topic of the cultural and social frameworks within which formulaic speech occurs, one further matter needs to be explored and that is the "licensing" of formulaic expressions. The processes by which an expression becomes socially licensed are as complex as the acceptance of any other social practice. If we look at auctions not just as verbal events but as social events, we can note that they consist of a rich system of beliefs and practices (Smith, 1989). Some of these are very general and may have been part of auctioning practice for centuries; others have grown up in particular commodity markets; and still others form part of the social fabric of a particular auction house. In each case, they have started as innovations of particular people. Over a period of time they have become part of the way things are done. Some of them are subject to change. Others appear to persist. In these ways, social practices and formulae are essentially the same.

EXPLANATIONS

At this point I return to the two questions that began this investigation: the question of what makes speech appropriate to a given situational context yet allows for it to be creative, and what makes human beings able to speak in real time. Turning first to the question of appropriateness and creativity, I have shown that formulae are indexed either for discourse roles or sociocultural roles. I am assuming that the former is a subset of the latter. When a speaker uses a formula in the role for which it is indexed, this makes speech at the moment of utterance appropriate. I have also shown that formulae frequently have variant forms given by tracks through a finite state diagram. Furthermore, in many situations there are a number of formulae that are indexed to that discourse or sociocultural role. The existence of multiple options allows for a measure of novelty.

Putting it slightly differently, a formulaic tradition makes available a restricted set of linguistic resources. The selection of these resources in a particular instance is related to the speaker's perception of what is required to be done. Thus, the tradition allows both for those aspects of the situation that are the same for all comparable situations to be given expression, as well as for those aspects of the situation that are unique. For example, in providing commentary for a horse race, formulae allow for the specific distance the race still has to run to be inserted. They allow for the specific names of horses to be inserted. But the continuity of horse races, their cyclic and linear natures, are also given expression in the discourse structure rules and the specific formulae dealing with the starts and finishes of races.

So speech in an oral formulaic tradition will be appropriate. If formulae are indexed either to discourse structure rules or to socially determined conditions for their use, then their use in the nonlinguistic contexts for which they are indexed must be appropriate. That is, the tradition defines appropriate speaking. For the uninitiated, race calls, cricket commentaries, and auctions are often unintelligible. Because every formula is discourse indexed, someone who does not knows the tradition to which it belongs will not know what the formula means, the context in which it is appropriate, or what it communicates. Such a person can only guess.

It can be seen that this is a specific hypothesis that runs parallel to what Malinowski and Firth had to say about speech in chapter 1.

But does this really leave room for novelty? Let us suppose that a sentence is *maximally novel* if a speaker has composed it entirely from the minimal units from which it may be composed. An English sentence is maximally novel if it is composed of words each selected individually. Maximal novelty assumes a particular balance between lexical lookup and speech processing. It assumes that the speaker looks up individual words, and then strings these words together using processing techniques. Maximal novelty therefore places the maximum load on syntactic and articulatory processing, and an equally great load on lookup of all the lexical items. *Minimal novelty,* by contrast, occurs in sentence production where the whole sentence is looked up from memory and spoken verbatim. Such novelty requires the minimum amount of processing and places the maximum amount of load on lexical lookup. Maximum novelty requires at least the lookup of words and perhaps such things as their grammatical endings (e.g., the plural or past tense ending). Minimal novelty requires at least the processing of the articulatory programming to speak the sentence. For example, there must be motor commands that tell the lips and tongue exactly what to do to produce a certain sequence of sounds. In brief, speech with either maximum or minimum novelty cannot therefore be undertaken without a measure of both lookup and processing.

This gives a metric for evaluating novelty. If speech production were generally maximally novel, then the factors that bear on speech production explored in the previous chapters will go no further than the kind of restricted varieties examined so far. Previous investigation of human speech production generally favors and sometimes presupposes the maximally novel view of speech production. This is true of Levelt's (1989) account of speech production. However, not everyone takes this view: "It is very likely that much more of the talk that goes on is idiomatic than just those utterances that can't be analysed. The fact that we can analyse doesn't necessarily mean that we do" (Bolinger, 1975, p. 297). "I believe that a large part of our ability to get along well in a language is our facility with formulaic expressions" (Fillmore, 1979, p. 100).

However, whether or not speech is maximally novel is not something that can be assumed, as Malinowski and Firth do in the quotations from their work in chapter 1. It would seem that sometimes it is close to minimally novel and sometimes close to maximally novel. This suggests that there is no general case. What must be done instead is to investigate when speech is less than maximally or more than minimally novel. This investigation can be approached from two directions. First, we can see whether the kinds of working memory and processing constraints that affect the formulaic performers whose speech I have described also affect other speakers. For example, air traffic controllers perform other complex tasks when they are speaking. The theory of the previous chapters predicts that formulaic composition techniques will be widely used in such situations.

Second, we can look at the outcome of speech processing to see just how novel utterances actually are in a number of varieties of speech. We might guess that, because humans do many things with words that count as social actions or have social and cultural significance, speech may be formulaic in many such contexts. For example, I would predict that elements of formulaic speech would be in evidence in situations that are politically volatile and in which a word out of place could land a speaker in prison. Formulaic speech may, in such a context, be a particular safe kind of speech.

Only by transcribing speech and understanding its context as it impinges on the speaker and hearer can we come to empirically based conclusions about just what people actually do when they speak and just how novel they are when speaking. It is important again to note that speakers always have at their disposal the resources that enable them to be maximally novel. But they also have available resources that allow them to speak in a less than maximally novel way. This latter possibility comes about because a language makes available conventional ways of expression. The data on which this study is based show that less than maximally novel speech is the norm in a number of routine contexts. I am suggesting it may be pervasive in society.

In answer to the second general question posed in chapter 1 of how it is that humans are able to speak in real time, I have shown that, under many different circumstances some or all of the properties of formulaic speech are resorted to in order to cut down the options made available by the speaker's internalized grammar. This is done largely by replacing syntactic processing by lexical lookup. Cutting down the options must assist with real-time processing of speech because having fewer options involves less processing. Less processing provides speakers with more time to do the processing that must be done. Because I assume, with Bresnan (1981), "that it is easier for us to look something up than to compute it" (p. 14), then formulaic speech creates opportunities for reducing computation by reading larger than one-word chunks out of memory. This creates more processing time for speech planning. In turn, this makes real-time speech processing easier in some circumstances and perhaps even possible in others. Speech perception also takes place in real time. Lookup of fragments longer than one word may also facilitate real-time speech perception by making speech more predictable.

It can be seen that this hypothesis is a version of the Parry and Lord hypothesis quoted in chapter 1. The answers I have come up with in this study also strongly echo those of Pawley and Syder (1983) in their investigation of the problems of nativelike selection and nativelike fluency, namely, how native speakers come in many contexts to select some expressions as more nativelike than others, and how native speakers come to be fluent. To be a native speaker under real-time pressures involves the use of formulaic resources.

CONCLUSION

Every speaker, every performer in a speech community, uses traditional resources. That is one of the things that makes us native speakers in our own communities rather than foreigners. Those who are the best speakers, the most fluent, the most impressive, the ones held in highest regard, are those who command a wide range of such resources and use them creatively, playing with them, bringing out arcane, little known expressions at exactly the right time in an appropriate context, creating new resources for their speech traditions. Attaining such a mastery over the speech traditions of a community is no different in a literate society than in a nonliterate society. The person who can speak fluently and appropriately in a meeting, who can entertain friends at a dinner party or a bar with well-selected and polished anecdotes must, perforce, be a practiced and mature performer, a smooth talker. In this sense, all societies are oral societies and all oral performers are heirs to oral traditions and all oral performers are evaluated for their performance, whether it be as auctioneer, friend, foe, employer, or job applicant. To understand all these roles speakers may fill, the traditional oral resources to which speakers are heirs must be understood. Then it must also be understood that every performer is an individual performer using traditional resources in his or her own personal ways. The resources themselves appear to evolve in response to psychological pressure speakers are under when they speak, namely restricted memory and processing resources. They are also a response to the necessity for social beings to behave in ways that are, in large part, socially appropriate. Formulaic speech fulfills both requirements.

Appendix

DATA COLLECTION AND ANALYSIS

The descriptions of nonlinguistic contexts for the studies contained in this book involved periods of field work. The approach I adopted was that of participant observer for at least some of the time. One can attend auctions without being observed to be anything other than an attender at auctions. I also listened to sports commentaries as anyone might. At other times I attended auctions as a linguist with a portable tape recorder (a Sony TC-D5M) and a directional microphone (an AKG D900). At such times I was still an observer but a rather abnormal participant. Auctiongoers normally thought I was from the media. The auctioneers had given permission for me to record under the normal requirement of informed consent. Sports commentaries were recorded off-air, usually on the same tape recorder.

The linguistic analysis of the recorded material involved making trancripts of the recordings and then analyzing them for distinctive linguistic features, that is, features that were distinctive of the particular register under observation, particularly for the features of discourse structure, formulae, prosodics, and hesitation phenomena. Formulae were collected on cards and grouped together by discourse function. Some were later analyzed for their finite state properties. In the case of one sample of livestock auctions, a detailed prosodic analysis was performed.

DATA SOURCES FOR *SMOOTH TALKERS*

Not all the data that form the observational underpinnings for this study have been recorded or transcribed. Formulaic performance is often so stereotyped that after field observation and listening to tape recordings, one or two characteristic tracks are all that are required to gain a representative analysis of the data.

In the following list I have indicated data sources that form the direct observational base for *Smooth Talkers,* as well as data that are more indirectly relevant.

All of the tapes from one field trip to the United States were stolen on my way back to New Zealand. However, I had already done some work on transcription and analysis before the tapes were stolen. Fortunately, replacement recordings of some of the auctioneers whom I had recorded were generously given to me by the R. J. Reynolds Tobacco Company, Billy Yeargin of Oxford, North Carolina, and Geoffrey M. Miller of Kingston, New York.

I.   Sports commentaries:
   A. Race callers:
      1. Tape recordings:
         a. 46 races off-air from Radio New Zealand in 1986 by J.P.M. Austin.
         b. Nine races ranging from 1935 to 1987 supplied by Radio New Zealand.
      2. Transcription:
        Transcriptions of (a) done by Peter Kane.
        Transcriptions of (b) done by Koenraad Kuiper.
   B. Cricket commentators:
      Sources: Crystal and Davy (1969); Pawley (1991)
   C. Ice hockey faceoff commentators:
      1. Tape recordings:
        Three NHL games recorded on November 26, December 3, and December 10, 1983 by the Canadian Broadcasting Corporation and provided by them to the author.
      2. Transcriptions:
        Selective transcription by Koenraad Kuiper.
II. Auctioneers:
   A. Real estate:
      1. Tape recordings:
         a. One of Rod Cameron of Wrightson NMA, March 11, 1982.
         b. 12 of various Christchurch auctioneers made by Heidi Quinn, 1993.
      2. Transcriptions:
        Transcription of (a) done by Koenraad Kuiper.
        Transcriptions of (b) done by Heidi Quinn.
        Transcriptions of Melbourne, Australia real estate auctions by Elizabeth Harris.
   B. Tobacco:
      1. Tape recordings:
         a. About 100 of auctions at Fuquay-Varina, North Carolina, 1981, performed by Hank Currin and Earl Capps, made by Koenraad Kuiper and subsequently stolen.
         b. Numerous auctions recorded over 2 days at the first world tobacco auctioning championships at Danville, Virginia, 1981, also stolen.

      c. Some replacement recordings of (b) provided by R. J. Reynolds and Billy Yeargin of Oxford, North Carolina.

      d. A number of old-time tobacco auctioneers. Tape provided by Billy Yeargin of Oxford, North Carolina.

  2. Transcriptions:

      Sample transcriptions of (a), (b), and (d) done by Koenraad Kuiper.

      Musical transcriptions of samples of (a) and (b) done by Frederick Tillis, The University of Massachusetts at Amherst.

C. Antique and general:

  1. Tape recordings:

      a. 20 auctions of Oriental carpets at Sotheby's in Belgravia, London, recorded by D. C. Haggo, June 1, 1982

      b. Milt Crosby of New York State recorded by Geoffrey M. Miller, December 6, 1980.

      c. Douglas Bilodeau of Deerfield, Massachusetts, recorded by Koenraad Kuiper, 1981.

         Replacement recordings of (c) by Geoffrey Miller, made December 5, 1980.

      d. R. G. Bell of Kaiapoi, NZ, recorded by Koenraad Kuiper, April 7, 1982.

  2. Transcriptions:

      Selected transcriptions of (a), (c), and (d) done by Koenraad Kuiper.

D. Livestock:

  1. Tape recordings:

      a. Various auctioneers at Banbury, England recorded by D. C. Haggo, November 26, 1981.

      b. Various auctioneers at the Ontario Stock Yards recorded by D. C. Haggo, January 22, 1982.

      c. Milt Crosby at Whately, Massachusetts, recorded by Koenraad Kuiper, 1981, subsequently stolen.

      d. Various auctioneers in North Canterbury, NZ, recorded by Koenraad Kuiper, 1977–1982.

  2. Transcriptions:

      Selected transcriptions of (a) and (b) done by D. C. Haggo.

      Selected transcriptions of (d) done by Koenraad Kuiper.

E. Produce:

  1. Tape recordings:

      Various auctioneers at McFarlane and Growers, Christchurch, NZ recorded by Koenraad Kuiper, May 5, 1982.

  2. Transcriptions:

      Selected transcriptions done by Koenraad Kuiper.

F. Wool:

  1. Tape recordings:

Various auctioneers at the Christchurch wool exchange, May 21, 1983.
2. Transcriptions:
Selected transcriptions done by Koenraad Kuiper.

TRANSCRIPTION

The transcriptions contained in this book are minimal in what they display of the complexities of speech. They are that way because they aim only to illustrate a limited array of linguistic facts, specifically discourse structure and formulae; sometimes, and to a lesser extent, pausing. More elaborate phonemic and prosodic transcriptions have been done for some of these recordings. However, what they display is not relevant to the present discussion.

References

Abrahams, R. D. (1970). *Deep down in the jungle...: Negro narrative folklore from the streets of Philadelphia.* Chicago: Aldine.

Abrahams, R. D. (1972). The training of the man of words in talking sweet. *Language in Society, 1,* 15–29.

Austin, J. L. (1976). *How to do things with words.* London: Oxford University Press.

Bauman, R. (1975). Verbal art as performance. *American Anthropologist, 77,* 290–311.

Bauman, R. (1986). *Story, performance, and event.* Cambridge, UK: Cambridge University Press.

Bell, A., & Holmes, J. (Eds.). (1990). *New Zealand ways of speaking English.* Bristol, UK: Multilingual Matters.

Biber, D., & Finegan, E. (Ed.). (1993). *Perspectives on register: Situating register variation within sociolinguistics.* New York: Oxford University Press.

Bolinger, D. (1975). *Aspects of language* (2nd ed.). New York: Harcourt, Brace, Jovanovich.

Bresnan, J. (1981). A realistic transformational grammar. In M. Halle, J. Bresnan, & G. A. Miller (Eds.), *Linguistic theory and psychological reality* (pp. 1–59). Cambridge, MA: MIT Press.

Cassady, R. (1967). *Auctions and auctioneering.* Berkeley: University of California Press.

Chafe, W. L. (1968). Idiomaticity as an anomaly in the Chomskian paradigm. *Foundations of Language, 4,* 109–127.

Chomsky, N. (1965). *Aspects of the theory of syntax.* Cambridge, MA: MIT Press.

Coulmas, F. (1979). On the sociolinguistic relevance of routine formulae. *Journal of Pragmatics, 3,* 239–266.

Coulmas, F. (Ed.). (1981). *Conversational routine: Explorations in standardized communication situations and prepatterned speech.* The Hague: Mouton.

Crystal, D. (1969). *Prosodic systems and intonation in English.* Cambridge, UK: Cambridge University Press.

Crystal, D., & Davy, D. (1969). *Investigating English style.* London: Longman.

Di Sciullo, A.-M., & Williams, E. (1987). *On the definition of word.* Cambridge, MA: MIT Press.

Edwards, V., & Sienkewicz, T. J. (1990). *Oral cultures past and present: Rappin and Homer.* Oxford, UK: Basil Blackwell.

Ferguson, C. (1976). The structure and use of politeness formulas. *Language in Society, 5,* 137–151.

Ferguson, C. (1983). Sports announcer talk: Syntactic aspects of register variation. *Language in Society, 12,* 153–172.

Fillmore, C. J. (1979). On fluency. In C. J. Fillmore, D. Kempler, & W. S.-Y. Wang (Eds.), *Individual differences in language ability and language behaviour* (pp. 85–101). New York: Academic Press.

Finnegan, R. (1981). Literacy and literature. In B. Lloyd & J. Gay (Eds.), *Universals of human thought* (pp. 234–255). Cambridge, UK: Cambridge University Press.

Firth, J. R. (1964). *Tongues of men and speech.* Oxford, UK: Oxford University Press.

Flindall, M. (1991). *Checkout operators: Formulae and oral traditions.* Unpublished manuscript, University of Canterbury, New Zealand.

Fodor, J. A., Bever, T. G., & Garrett, M. F. (1974). *The psychology of language.* New York: McGraw-Hill.

Fraser, B. (1970). Idioms within a transformational grammar. *Foundations of Language, 6,* 22–42.

Frazier, L. (1979). *On comprehending sentences.* Bloomington: Indiana University Linguistics Club.

Haggo, D. C., & Kuiper, K. (1985). Stock auction speech in Canada and New Zealand. In R. Berry & J. Acheson (Eds.), *Regionalism and national identity: Multidisciplinary essays on Canada, Australia and New Zealand* (pp. 189–197). Christchurch: Association for Canadian Studies in Australia and New Zealand.

Harrah, J. (1992). *The landscape of possibility: An ethnography of the Kentucky Derby.* Unpublished doctoral dissertation, Indiana University, Bloomington.

Harris, E. P. (1993). *Auction this day: An ethnography of auction sale communication. The situation in Melbourne, Australia.* Unpublished doctoral dissertation, La Trobe University, Australia.

Hawkins, D. N. (1957). *Beyond the Waimakariri.* Christchurch: Whitcombe & Tombs.

Herdt, G. H. (1980). *The guardians of the flutes.* New York: Macmillan.

Hickey, F. (1991) *What Penelope said: Styling the weather forecast.* Unpublished master's thesis, University of Canterbury, New Zealand.

Holmes, J. (1992). *An introduction to sociolinguistics.* London: Longman.

Hymes, D. (1968). The ethnography of speaking. In J. Fishman (Ed.), *The sociology of language* (pp. 99–138). The Hague: Mouton.

Ji, F.-Y., Kuiper, K., & Shu, S.-G. (1990). Language and revolution: Formulae of the Chinese cultural revolution. *Language and Society, 19,* 61–79.

Koenig, E. (1972). The cattle auctions in central Texas. *Folklore Annual, 2,* 60–77.

Kuiper, A. C. (1986). *If you think you can do it, then go for it: Women in apprenticeships.* Christchurch, New Zealand: Christchurch Polytechnic.

Kuiper, K. (1990). New Zealand sporting formulae: Two models of male socialisation. In J. Cheshire (Ed.), *English around the world: Sociolinguistic perspectives* (pp. 200–209). Cambridge, UK: Cambridge University Press.

Kuiper, K. (1991). The evolution of an oral tradition: Racecalling in Canterbury, New Zealand. *Oral Tradition, 6,* 19–34.

Kuiper, K. (1994). A short dictionary of livestock auction formulae collected at North Canterbury livestock auctions. *New Zealand English Newsletter, 8,* 11–17.

Kuiper, K., & Austin, J. P. M. (1990). They're off and racing now: The speech of the New Zealand race caller. In A. Bell & J. Holmes (Eds.), *New Zealand ways of speaking English* (pp. 195–220). Bristol, UK: Multilingual Matters.

Kuiper, K., & Haggo, D. C. (1984). Livestock auctions, oral poetry and ordinary language. *Language and Society, 13,* 205–234.

Kuiper, K., & Haggo, D. C. (1985). The nature of ice hockey commentaries. In R. Berry & J. Acheson (Eds.), *Regionalism and national identity: Multidisciplinary essays on Canada, Australia and New Zealand* (pp. 167–175). Christchurch: Association for Canadian Studies in Australia and New Zealand.

Kuiper, K., & Tillis, F. (1986). The chant of the tobacco auctioneer. *American Speech, 60,* 141–149.

Langendoen, J. T. (1968). *The London school of linguistics: A study in the linguistic theories of B. Malinowski and J.R. Firth.* Cambridge, MA: MIT Press.

Levelt, M, W. J. (1989). *Speaking: From intention to articulation.* Cambridge, MA: MIT Press.

Lord, A. B. (1960). *The singer of tales.* Cambridge, MA: Harvard University Press.

Malinowski, B. (1922). *Argonauts of the western Pacific.* London: Routledge & Kegan Paul.

Mandelbaum, D. G. (Ed.). (1958). *Selected writings of Edward Sapir.* Berkeley: University of California Press.

Manes, J., & Wolfson, N. (1981). The compliment formula. In F. Coulmas (Ed.), *Conversational routine* (pp. 115–132). The Hague: Mouton.

Miller, G. A. (1956). The magical number 7, plus or minus two: Some limits of our capacity for processing information. *Psychological Review, 3,* 81–97.

106

Miller, G. M. (1984). "Are you unhappy at a twenty dollar bill?": Text, tune and context at antique auctions. *Ethnomusicology, 28,* 187–208.

Mitkov, R. (1991). Generating public weather reports. In *International conference on current issues in computational linguistics* (pp. 419–425). Penang, Malaysia: Universiti Sains Malasia.

Newell, A., & Simon, H. A. (1972). *Human problem solving.* Englewood Cliffs, NJ: Prentice-Hall.

Newton-Smith, W. H. (1981). *The rationality of science.* London: Routledge & Kegan Paul.

Parry, M. (1930). Studies in the epic technique of oral verse-making. I: Homer and Homeric style. *Harvard Studies in Classical Philology, 41,* 73–147.

Parry, M. (1932). Studies in the epic technique of oral verse-making. II: The Homeric language as the language of an oral poetry. *Harvard Studies in Classical Philology, 43,* 1–50.

Pawley, A. (1991). How to talk cricket. In R. Blust (Ed.), *Currents in Pacific linguistics: Papers in austronesian languages and ethnolinguistics in honour of George W. Grace* (pp. 339–368). Honolulu, HI: Pacific Linguistics.

Pawley, A., & Syder, F. (1983). Two puzzles for linguistic theory: Nativelike selection and nativelike fluency. In J. Richards & R. Schmidt (Eds.), *Language and communication* (pp. 191–226). London: Longman.

Peterson, S., & Georgianna, D. (1988). New Bedford's fish auction: A study in auction method and market power. *Human Organisation, 47,* 235–241.

Popper, K. R. (1965). *The logic of scientific discovery.* New York: Harper & Row.

Powell, R. (1961). *The law of agency.* London: Pitman.

Rosaldo, M. Z. (1980). The use and abuse of anthropology: Reflections on feminism and cross cultural understanding. *Signs, 5,* 389–417.

Rosenberg, B. A. (1970). The formulaic quality of spontaneous sermons. *Journal of American Folklore, 83,* 3–20.

Salmond, A. (1975). *Hui: A study of Maori ceremonial gatherings.* Cambridge, UK: Cambridge University Press.

Smith, C. W. (1989). *Auctions: The social construction of value.* London: Harvester Wheatsheaf.

Treitel, G. H. (1970). *The law of contract.* London: Stephens.

Wanta, W., & Meggett, D. (1988). "Hitting paydirt": Capacity theory and sports announcers' use of clichés. *Journal of Communication, 38,* 82–89.

Weinreich, U. (1969). Problems in the analysis of idioms. In J. Puhvel (Ed.), *Substance and the structure of language* (pp. 23–81). Berkeley: University of California Press.

Yaghi, H. M. (1994). *A psycholinguistic model of simultaneous translation, and proficiency assessment by automated acoustic analysis of discourse.* Unpublished doctoral dissertation, University of Auckland, Auckland, New Zealand.

Zanetti, B. (1991). Towards a non-sexist language: A preliminary survey and analysis of lingular *they* use in New Zealand English. *New Zealand English Newsletter, 5,* 26–34.

Author Index

Levelt, M. W. J., 2, 97
Lord, A. B., 5, 88

M

Malinowski, B., 4
Manes, J., 93, 94
Meggett, D., 31
Miller, G. A., 29
Miller, G. M., 51, 88
Mitkov, R., 91

N

Newell, A., 29
Newton-Smith, W. H., 1

P

Parry, M., 5
Pawley, A., 3, 23, 92, 98
Peterson, S., 35
Popper, K. R., 1
Powell, R., 36

R

Rosaldo, M. Z., 88
Rosenberg, B. A., 90

S

Salmond, A., 87
Sapir, E., 95
Shu, S.-G., 94
Sienkewicz, T. J., 90
Simon, H. A., 29
Smith, C. W., 34, 35, 95
Syder, F., 3, 92, 98

T

Tillis, F., 51
Treitel, G. H., 36

W

Wanta, W., 31
Weinreich, U., 45
Williams, E., 45
Wolfson, N., 93, 94

Y

Yaghi, H. M., 9

Z

Zanetti, B., xi

Subject Index

109

data sources, 100–103
interdisciplinary, 1–2
transcription, 103

O

Oral traditions
acquisition of, 80, 81–83
as cultural artifacts, 88–89
evolution of, 74–80
gendered nature of, ix, 87–88
mastery of, 84–87

P

Perception
acculturated nature of, 27–29
Performance
appropriate, 96
creativity, 5, 86–87
definitions, 1–3
novelty, 96–98
psychological aspects, 2–5, 98
sociocultural aspects, 2–3, 5–7

textual study of, 6–7

R

Ritual, 5–6
auctions, 34–36, 48–49, 51–52, 56–61, 64–65
definition of, 6
insults, 94–95
Routine, 5–6, 26
cricket, 22
definition of, 6
and discourse rules, 27–29
horse racing, 10–11

S

Speech acts, 92

W

Weather forecasting, 90–91
Writing, 90–91